EDITORIAL

In the last issue, we drew attention to the action taken by the Secretary of State for the Environment to commence the statutory protection of, among other categories of post-1939 buildings, certain Second World War defence sites. But as we said then, it is not enough simply to identify those of particular historic importance and to schedule or list them as most appropriate. Management in its broadest sense is essential to ensure their survival. With comparatively recent coastal defences and their all too frequently decaying reinforced-concrete and dangerous pitfalls, coastal batteries in particular have often been regarded as eyesores to be demolished and tidied away. There can therefore be nothing but praise for the initiative shown by Tendring District Council, Essex, in producing a handsomely printed draft action and management plan for Beacon Hill Battery at Harwich (*Director of Planning & Economic Development, Tendring District Council, Weeley, Clacton-on-Sea, Essex CO16 9AJ*). The document is intended to provide an opportunity for a wide range of responses from a number of organisations which have interests in ancient monuments and fortifications, local history, tourism and the town itself.

The document identifies Beacon Hill Battery's historic importance, both in its role in the long history of the defence of the estuary of the Stour and the Orwell, and as a prototype for other coastal batteries of the early 1890s in the adoption of the new doctrine of invisibility. Its main armament was to be one 10-inch and one 6-inch breech-loader mounted on hydro-pneumatic disappearing mountings with supporting armament of quick-firing guns. On its landward side, the battery was provided with a form of ditch defence known as the 'Twydall Profile', and, with its associated bombardment shelter, these are probably the earliest surviving examples in the country. The modifications to the battery during two World Wars are not without interest. The radar tower, with some of the internal aerial array still surviving, is one of the earliest radar emplacements in the country. Recognition of this level of historical importance is acknowledged to be due largely to the research of Charles Trollope and others of the Fortress Study Group.

The District Council owns only part of the site but its action plan suggests policies for the battery and its environs which can ensure long term preservation and public involvement. In its concern for wider conservation issues it has also sought the views of the Essex Naturalists Trust. This approach can serve as an example for other local authorities with potentially interesting coastal defence sites, and not least for English Heritage with its responsibilities for neighbouring Landguard Fort and similar sites elsewhere. The analysis of the different issues and the step by step development plan for selective reinstatement and presentation of the battery to the visitor owes much to Victor Smith, also of the Fortress Study Group. His initiative and experience in the careful restoration of New Tavern Fort, Gravesend and Coalhouse Fort, East Tilbury has demonstrated what can be achieved. Victor Smith describes his current research and restoration project at Brimstone Hill Fortress, St Kitts, elsewhere in this issue.

Beacon Hill – 6-inch Mk VII gun emplacement 1941-56, with radar tower beyond. (*Tendring DC*)

From Canada comes a similar consultation document. The first newsletter concerning the Historic Halifax Defence Complex, National Historic Sites, and published by the Canadian Parks Service, has for its theme the broad issue of a management plan for the future development of various forts in and around Halifax Harbour. This first issue is entitled 'Planning for the Future'. The Canadian Parks Service already has an approved Management Plan for the Halifax Citadel and the Director General of the Canadian Parks Service (Atlantic Region) has invited views on what can be done to protect and provide

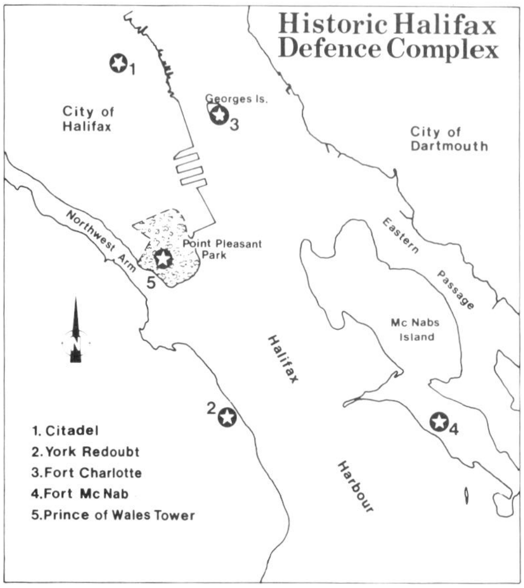

for the visitors' understanding of the rest of Halifax's historic defences: York Redoubt, Georges Island, Fort McNab, and the Prince of Wales Tower. The newsletter is obtainable from the Superintendent, Halifax Defence Complex, Canadian Parks Service, PO Box 1480, Halifax, Nova Scotia, B3K 5H7.

The newsletter sets out the historic importance of Halifax as one of the four principal British overseas naval stations along with Gibraltar, Malta and Bermuda and its role in imperial strategic planning during the eighteenth and nineteenth centuries. As a result, its defences include a complete conspectus of coastal defences from the late eighteenth century to the Second World War, and as such, is thought to be unique on the North American continent. There are short historical summaries of each of the sites together with simplified plans and photographs as well as future conservation options. York Redoubt began in the 1790s as an open battery with a martello tower built in 1798. The battery was completely reconstructed in the 1860s with the introduction of the rifled muzzle-loader but was obsolete by the late 1890s and was replaced by Somerset Battery. Fort Charlotte occupies the high ground of Georges Island and was also begun in the 1790s. By 1870 it was the key to the protection of the inner harbour and at the core of a submarine mining defence. Fort McNab was a product of the late 1880s and built for the new breech-loading guns. Prince of Wales Tower was begun in 1796 above the batteries below Point Pleasant Park on the Halifax peninsula. Some additional fortifications which lie outside this brief are also mentioned. There is also a summary of recent archaeological investigations.

We can report on the fourth annual meeting of the Castles Studies Group held in early April at Carrickfergus Castle, Northern Ireland and with a further two full days spent visiting castle sites in County Down and County Antrim. The eternal problem of how to distinguish native 'raised raths' from the mottes of the Anglo-Norman conquest was demonstrated by these field visits. The numerous Ulster mottes were virtually a hundred years later than those introduced into England after 1066. While their appearance is much the same, their functions had changed from those of their English counterparts and they seemed to have a more residential purpose than a purely military one. Much work in Ireland is currently directed towards the study of tower houses and led by Dr Terry Barry from Trinity College Dublin and Dr Tom Macneil from Queen's University, Belfast. There were presentations from several of their research students and from Dr Barry himself. There was evidence to support thirteenth century origins in some cases. To bring one to today's realities in Ireland, the scale and variety of the fortifications to protect such things as police stations and UDR barracks reminded those from outside the province that an aspect of the present 'troubles' is the continuing need for defensive works.

For those readers of *Fortress* travelling in Europe this summer, a visit to the Germanisches National Museum at Nuremberg for the exhibition in celebration of the eight hundredth anniversary of the Teutonic Order should provide an insight into the castles and military works of the Teutonic Knights. The exhibition is open from 30 June to 30 September.

In the current issue of *Fortress*, in addition to Victor Smith's article on Brimstone Hill Fortress, St Kitts, already mentioned, there is a description by Ken Denholm of the unusual defences begun by the English East India Company on the island of St Helena and continued after the island became a Crown Colony. Dale Floyd brings to our attention the batteries built by the US Army at Guantanamo, Cuba in the early years of this century. Jean Counihan, in an entirely different vein, explores the development of castle studies in England around the turn of the present century, and in particular the contribution to them of Mrs Ella Armitage. Finally, Sandy Gerrard keeps us up to date with an account of recent excavations at Carew Castle, Dyfed.

Andrew Saunders

CASTLES, CANNON AND CASEMATES

DR VOLKER SCHMIDTCHEN PROVIDES AN HISTORICAL SURVEY OF THE FUNDAMENTAL CHANGE IN MILITARY ARCHITECTURE IN THE FIFTEENTH AND SIXTEENTH CENTURIES.

In the first half of the fourteenth century a sound never heard before announced the end of the Middle Ages. This was the report of the first firearms: hand-guns and cannons. As had happened in previous periods in the history of mankind, a number of inventions within the sphere of military technology heralded a new era which in this case can perhaps be labelled 'Modern Times'.

THE BOMBARD REVOLUTION

The discovery and subsequent development of firearms in the fourteenth and through into the sixteenth century influenced the social, economic and political conditions of that period in a fashion which is paralleled by today's nuclear armaments race and maintenance of massive conventional forces. During this transitional period, the technical progress reflected by the development of firearms not only led to a complete change of military opinion on strategy and tactical formations, it also resulted in an expanding market for the raw materials needed for the production and for the use of these new weapons: iron to forge the guns, copper and tin for casting them, saltpetre, charcoal and sulphur (brimstone) to make the gunpowder.

Military architecture of this period of transition between the Middle Ages and 'Modern Times' is a major subject of interest. The evolution of the first heavy bombards of the fourteenth century into the more sophisticated siege artillery of the sixteenth century caused fundamental changes within the sphere of fortification. Most of the walls and towers of medieval castles and defended towns were no longer a match for the new and powerful firearms of the bombard type.

The wide range of medieval fortifications had previously only to face an arsenal of mechanically operated engines of war such as battering rams, stone-throwing catapults and trebuchets. The projectiles 'fired' by these various stone-throwing devices hit the walls and towers of the strongholds after following a high-angle trajectory, whereas those fired by a heavy piece of gunpowder ordnance – and until *c*1450 these too only used stone balls for ammunition – reached their target on a nearly flat trajectory, provided that the target lay within a suitable range of 300 to 500 metres. The balls fired by cannon struck their target at approximately right angles and with considerably higher penetrative force.

The 'Pumhart von Steyr', a giant stone-throwing bombard. The stone projectile had a diameter of 80cm (31½in). *(Heeresgeschtictliiches Museum, Vienna)*

Bronze stone-throwing mortar belonging to the Order of the Knights of St John, Rhodes, c1480. Overall length 190cm (75in); length of chamber 80cm (31½in; diameter of shot 45cm (15¾in); weight of shot 124kg (273lbs)

During the fourteenth to sixteenth centuries successful sieges across Europe demonstrated that this new type of weapon required a response in the field of military architecture. The ability to withstand this threat depended upon several factors: the topographical situation of the stronghold, capital resources in the form of finance, workforce, materials, and – most important –

Dardanelles gun (Tower of London). Overall length 518cm (204in); length of the chamber 215cm (84½ in); diameter of shot 63cm (25in); weight of shot 340kg (750lbs)

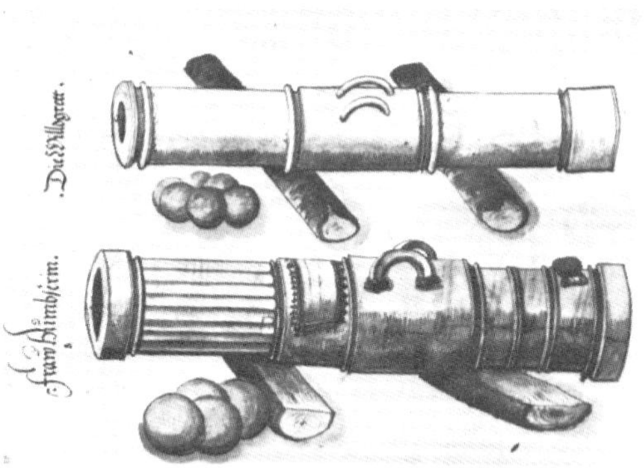

Stone-throwing bombards. (*Codex iconographicus Monacensis 222*)

the skill of available architects or military engineers. Only a few castles could be suitably reinforced but most fortified towns could undertake an extensive remodelling of their defences. The basic need was to strengthen the walls against the increased striking and penetrative capacity of cannon balls and to obtain larger spaces on top of the defences to deploy their own batteries.

SOCIAL CHANGES

Through continual experimentation, the skills and experience needed for the production of the new guns progressed steadily. This entailed the necessity for a division of labour and hence a certain degree of specialisation. So on the one hand, some 'experts' advanced from the status of simple craftsmen – blacksmiths or metal casters – to that of manufacturers of what were not only the most modern but even the ultimate weapons of the time. Such men were courted by kings and emperors and were richly recompensed. On the other hand, many formerly independent craftsmen lost their status and became dependent workers. Through this division of labour, the manufacturing process became more efficient, but normally the workers themselves had to concentrate only on one or two parts of the whole process, and with that 'specialisation', they lost many of their former qualifications. As they were concerned with mostly simple, and thus easily taught details of the process, the workers of a gun foundry, a forge or a gunpowder mill quickly became interchangeable.

Similarly, we have to consider the question of armaments from more than one angle. The race to achieve military superiority necessary for the promotion of one's own political aims is not an invention of our own times. A great deal of money has always been needed to achieve the striking capacity to forge ahead with such plans. From this point of view, it is hardly surprising that most of the knights – the previously much-admired military professionals, heroes of the crusades and idols of legendary tales – lost their importance as dreaded feudal warriors and the highest exponents of the medieval art of warfare. They usually depended on the agrarian produce and income of their feudal tenures, but with the late medieval economic crisis in Europe, they quite literally lost the ground under their feet. This economic decline was, however, but the first step on the way down. It was soon followed by the relinquishing of the ideals of knighthood, by taking service as mercenaries in the so-called free companies in France and Italy, or by becoming robber

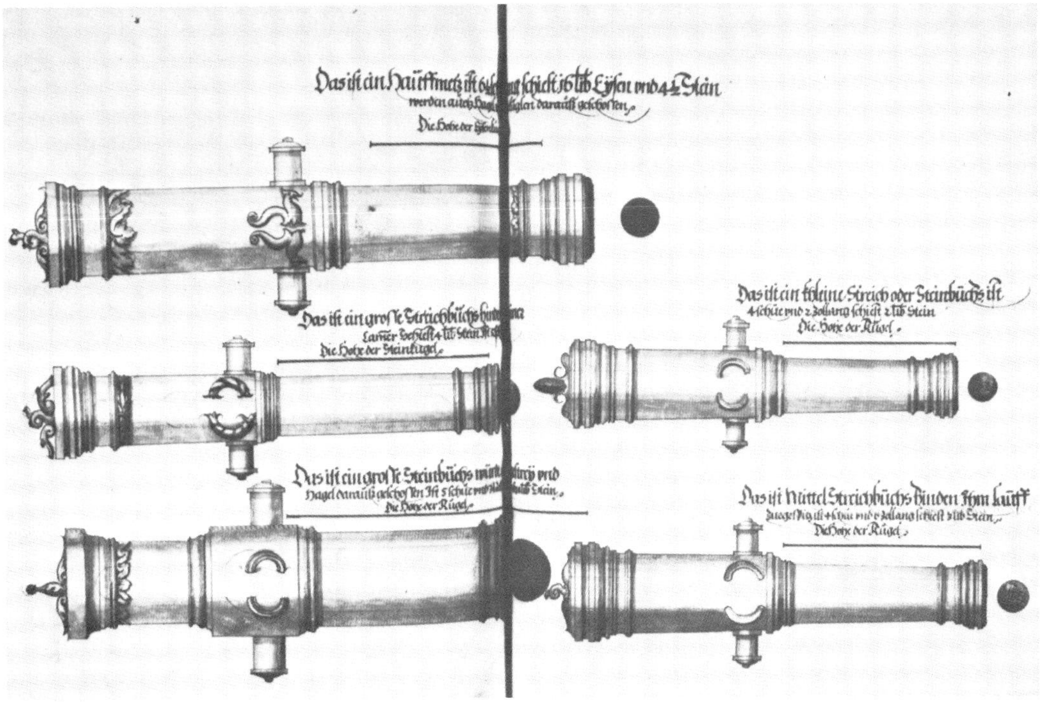

Cannon of the late sixteenth century. (*Codex germanicus Monacensis 8143*)

barons.

Some, however, understood that within the framework of the noticeable change in medieval European society – in Huizinga's phrase, the 'Autumn of the Middle Ages' – they had opportunities as servicemen to the powerful sovereigns of the rising territorial states, or as captains of the militia of the larger and richer cities, which derived their political importance from their economic power whether by trade or as rulers of territorial states with feudal rights over the exploitation of natural resources such as silver and copper mining, minting or the like.

EFFECTS ON DEFENSIVE ARCHITECTURE

There are many instances of the numerous and diverse consequences of the rise and development of firearms, but here I will consider one particular aspect of the subject: the reaction in the field of defensive architecture to this new type of military threat.

During the last decades of the fourteenth century, the effect of any military conflict, including sieges of castles and fortified towns, changed completely. For the first time besiegers had the opportunity of bringing heavy guns into action: the so-called bombards, wrought-iron cannons of enormous dimensions, capable of firing stone balls with a weight of 100lbs to 700lbs (45–320kg). In the fifteenth century, a number of successful sieges across Europe made it clear that the defenders simply had to devise new ways to strengthen their fortifications against this

Siege of Padua, 1509. (*Codex palaeographicus Vindobonensis 3032*)

new type of weapon. The most striking example of all was the fall of Constantinople on 29 May 1453. It resulted from the cannonade experienced by the city from the huge Turkish bombards, which by then were cast in bronze. To the minds of all contemporary military experts, Constantinople, with its 12m (40ft) high and 5m (16ft) thick walls, was reputed to be the strongest fortress in the world; so one can easily imagine how the news of its fall shocked Western Europe.

Meanwhile, technological development went on, leading to better guns and to a new type of ammunition, the iron ball. Another major disadvantage of the stone-firing heavy bombards which constituted the early siege artillery of the fourteenth and fifteenth centuries, was their lack of mobility. Transporting these guns was not the only problem. In order to get them into a correct firing position in front of a besieged stronghold these bombards had to be placed on the ground and anchored there by means of a bracing system of wooden beams in order to absorb

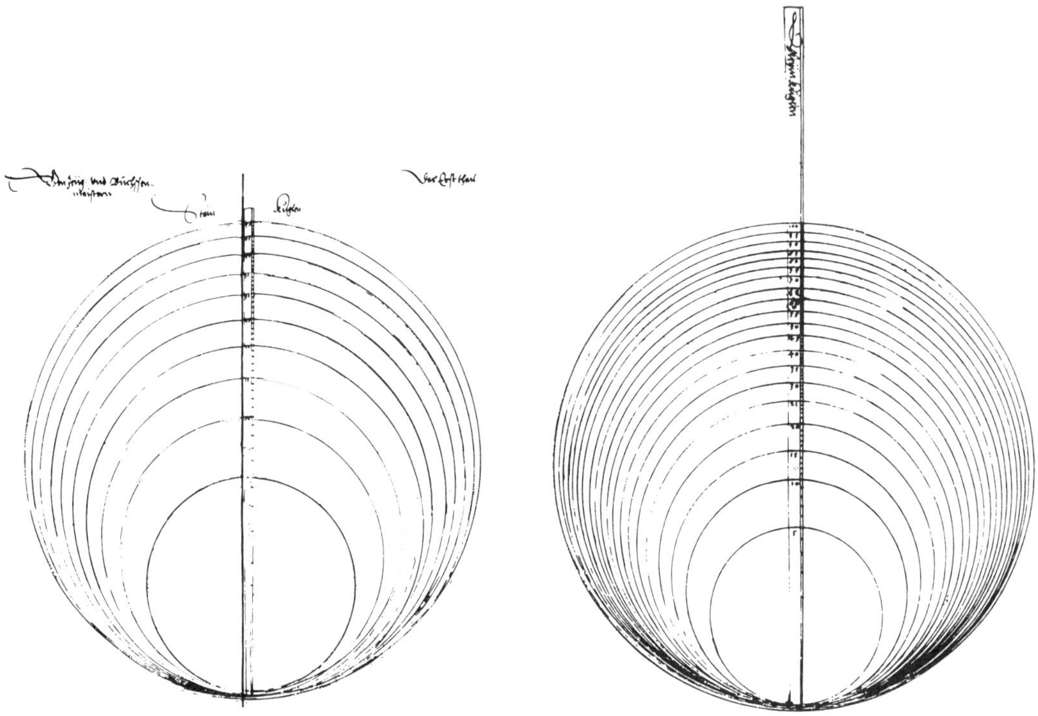

Stone (left) and lead cannon balls (right) drawn at the same scale in an artillery manual written c1570 by Leonhart Fronsperger. (*Codex palaeographicus Vindobensis 10.866*)

the recoil. Therefore, these bombards were always vulnerable to the threat of a quick sally by the besieged.

In the first half of the sixteenth century, the master gunners realized that iron has nearly three times the specific gravity of stone. Therefore, smaller sized cannons intended to fire iron balls could be forged in iron or cast in bronze while still maintaining the same striking power, or even augmenting it. Moreover, such cannons could be mounted on a wheeled gun carriage which greatly improved their mobility. The iron ball offered an additional advantage: it now became possible to forge or cast large numbers of such projectiles to standard sizes. Thus, it became possible to build up an effective stock of ammunition for cannon of various calibres.

The ability to withstand this new menace depended on several factors, among them the topographical situation of the stronghold, capital resources in men and materials and of course the ingenuity of the engineers. On the Continent, only a few of the castles could be reinforced in an adequate way. Nearly all those located on a plain lost their military significance, even if they had ditches and water defences. Indeed a moat might impede the action of a battering ram, but it did not provide any protection against cannon balls.

Until the late sixteenth century, only those castles located on top of hills or in a mountain area and reinforced with additional defences could still serve as effective strongholds (*eg* the Hohkönigsburg in the Vosges region). Most of the fortified towns, however, were able to undertake extensive remodelling of their circumvallation. The first requirement was to consolidate the weaker points of the defences, such as the curtain walls, the gates, and even some of the towers. But when trying to assess the effort which both smaller towns and larger cities made to withstand the threat of the powerful guns of possible besiegers, we should also take into account a few other important factors, such as the number of fighting men available for the defence of the walls, and the morale of the citizens.

The inhabitants had a duty to keep up the town defences in peacetime and, in case of war, to serve either on the fortifications or as members of the urban levy present on the battlefield. Morale depended on the degree of conviction that defence was necessary. There was a difference between the strict loyalty of the followers and household of a noble lord of a castle on the one hand, and the often strongly diverging interests of the members of an urban community on the other. Thus, it could happen that the majority of the citizens might feel that surrender was the best protection against the risks and consequences attendant upon a siege.

DEFENSIVE CHANGES

Many municipal authorities therefore tried to reinforce the defences of towns in such a way that such negative attitudes of the citizenry were not allowed to develop. This meant that the authorities went to enormous lengths to

strengthen their fortifications with the intention both of deterring the possible aggressor and of forestalling any internal discussion on surrender. Looking at the fifteenth and sixteenth town defences today, we have to distinguish two phases: the first is that of the remodelling of the existing medieval defences; the second is that of the building of bastioned fortifications based on earthwork ramparts and with dry or floodable ditches. The common aim was to improve the resistance capacity of the defences while at the same time gaining space on and within the fortifications in order to assemble and deploy one's own guns most effectively.

In the absence of a better technical solution, the first step was to make the traditional medieval walls thicker and the towers stronger. Thus, for instance, Robert de la Marche decided to build walls 6m (20ft) thick at Hasbain Castle; so did the architects who constructed the angle turrets of the castle at Naples; the Count of St Pol ordered a keep with 10m (32ft) thick walls to be built at Ham Castle.

A more progressive development involved additions to, and reinforcement of, medieval defences. Earthwork ramparts were constructed against the inner face of the existing walls or sometimes piled against the outer side. As a result, the upper part of the defences grew broader and, after the former (often wooden) wall passages had been removed, there was room enough to assemble one's own garrison batteries. The military engineers originally thought that by throwing up a rampart against the inner side of the wall it provided additional protection since, if the besiegers' artillery should breach the wall, there would be a further earthwork obstacle. Throughout the fifteenth century,

Siege of a strongly fortified hill-fortress at the end of the fifteenth century. (*Codex palatinus germanicus 126*)

The storming of a town following battery by siege artillery. (*Codex palaeographicus Vindobensis 3032*)

Top: master gunner aiming a cannon for a direct shot at a nearby objective by looking along the highest points of the barrel.
Centre: aiming at a distant objective by means of a handspike.
Bottom: aiming a cannon at an objective which lies lower; the gunner uses a spike at the muzzle and holds a ladle. (*Codex palaeolographicus Vindobensis 10.952*)

however, practical experience in fact demonstrated that when the wall was breached the inner rampart tumbled into the breach thus providing an easy way of ascent for the assaulting troops.

Therefore, the engineers responsible for strengthening town defences – where, in contrast to most castles, they had more room to add new elements of fortification – preferred embanking the outer face of the walls especially on those sides most vulnerable to attack. This type of rampart in fact provided additional protection against the besieging artillery because the earth absorbed the kinetic energy of the projectiles, and reduced their penetration capacity almost entirely. Under these circumstances, breaching the walls became far more difficult.

Another way to reinforce traditional medieval defences was to provide *fausse-brayes* or 'shot-traps' consisting of a low breastwork or bank at the foot of the walls. Medieval town defences, as well as a few castles, sometimes had outworks or a barbican consisting of the space between the lower *fausse-brayes* and the higher curtain wall. In the Middle Ages this space was often used as a bear-pit. It was not at all difficult to reinforce this defence system. A deep ditch was dug immediately in front of the *fausse-braye* and the resulting spoil was used to raise the level inside a barbican. This not only provided better protection for the earlier circular wall of the barbican but it was also a more suitable platform for guns. If a *fausse-braye* did not exist,

Master gunner aiming by means of a hand quadrant. (*Codex paleolographicus Vindobensis 10.891*)

such a rampart was often constructed. In that case, an additional ditch generally separated this rampart from the main enceinte. The *fausse-braye* ran parallel to the latter, projecting forward at the gates to form a kind of bulwark. Such bastion-like bulwarks then made flanking fire more effective.

Ditches played a role which gradually and consistently grew more important. This was particularly true in the case of urban defences. They constituted obstacles which the besiegers had to take seriously, especially when the moats were given the additional protection offered by casemated guns firing through embrasures located between the projecting bulwarks and the gate defences in the walled enceinte. These casemates might provide a covered passage-way for the defenders if the latter wanted to reach the outer defences safely. As flanking units armed with a few light guns, they also made it possible to enfilade the moat from both sides. In the sixteenth century, these flanking units became adapted to form caponiers designed for guns, even if a covered and protected passage-way was not required.

During this period caponiers developed into a component of fortification which was to become typical of later periods. The besiegers had first to eliminate these ditch defending caponiers before they could attempt the assault on the main ramparts. Thus, the defenders gained additional time to concert their own responses to the attack.

In spite of all the rebuilding and reinforcing of the existing fortifications, the basic structure of medieval military architecture with its main components of moat, wall and towers remained essentially the same throughout the fifteenth century. Using *fausse-brayes* and bulwarks, military engineers succeeded in creating a line of defence in front of the main fortifications. But still the visible high towers and curtain wall, which were increasingly vulnerable to the besiegers' artillery precisely because of their height, now became the weaker points of the stronghold.

By contrast to what was to develop first in Italy and then in France, the architect/engineers working in the Holy Roman Empire did not want to abandon the old defensive principle of super-elevation. Yet only by reducing the height of the towers and walls when constructing new defences in front of the stronghold could the defenders conceal the main defensive components from the sight of the besiegers and therefore also from their artillery.

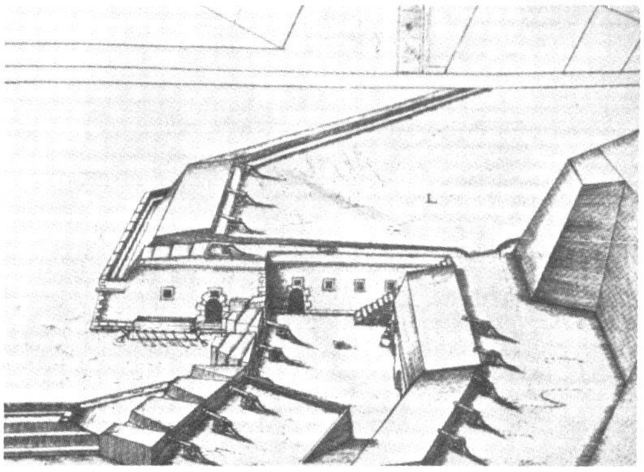

Sixteenth century fortification with *fausse-braye* (by Speckle 1589)

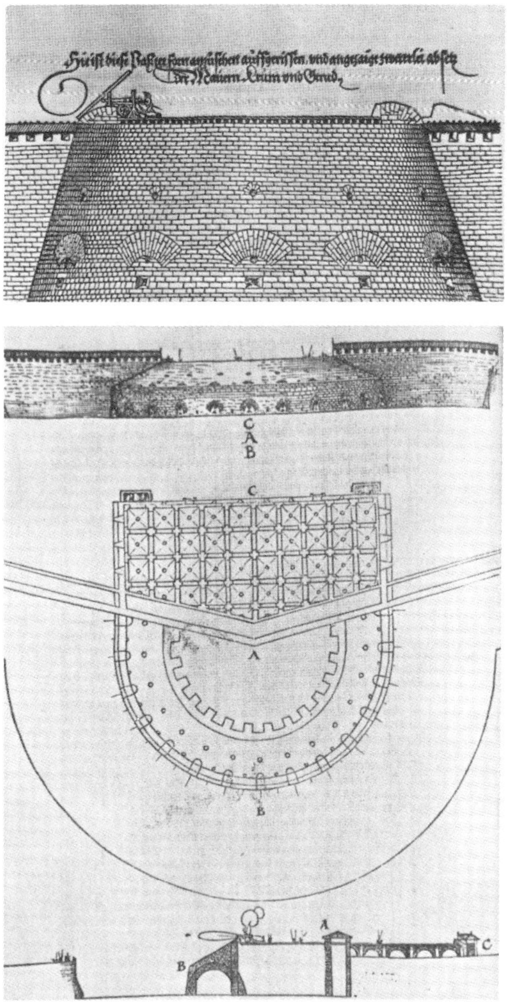

Durer's bastion in plan and section (1527)

THE MOVE TOWARDS THE BASTION SYSTEM AND ITS SUBSEQUENT DEMISE

From the medieval castle and town walls to the angle bastioned fortresses of the sixteenth century which evolved through distinctive design forms from the Old to New Italian, and later from the Old to New Dutch (including various modifications), the whole development of military architecture was no more than a step-by-step process which followed that of the guns; from the first heavy bombards of the fourteenth century to siege artillery as an autonomous military branch in

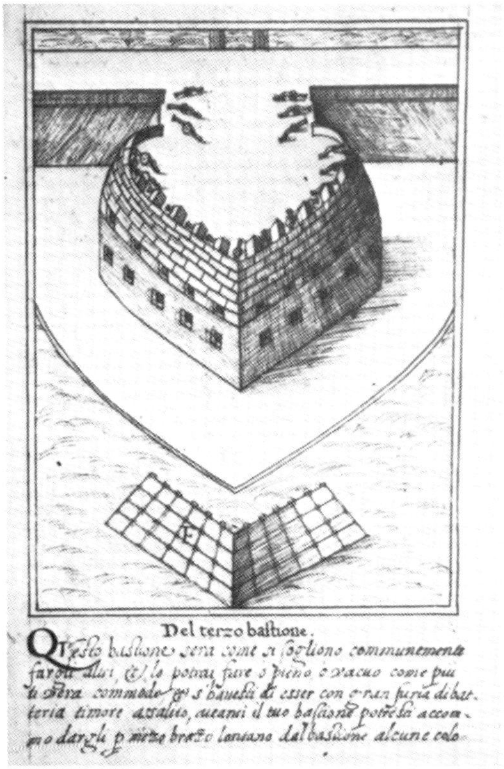

Italian bastion c1550; heart-shaped and with casemates. (*Codex palaeographicus Vindobensis 10.866*)

the sixteenth century.

This slow development is explained by the fact that all the efforts spent in planning and constructing new fortifications were basically nothing more than reactions to the successive new threats presented by the arrival of more advanced and better guns. In this respect, it should not be forgotten that the technique of printing was not invented until the middle of the fifteenth century. Before that time a rapid and widely spread transfer of knowledge was impossible. The diffusion of new ideas and of new solutions to commonly experienced problems always depends on the nature and quality of the information media. So it is not surprising that the first substantive book on the art of fortification was not published before the mid-sixteenth century. Before that time, ideas and inventions were communicated from father to son, from master to student.

As a result, the first phase in the development of modern fortification was characterised by the well concealed and private knowledge of a few famous architects such as Leonardo da Vinci, Francesco di Giorgio Martini, Alphonso Adriano, Carlo Theti, Francesco Marchi, Michele Sanmicheli, Niccolo Tartaglia, Bonaiuto Lorini, the Pasqualini brothers, Daniel Speckle and others. The example of newly built fortresses made this knowledge more widely understood and this explains why for nearly a century only modifications of the basic concept can be identified since progress was largely maintained by adapting from visible examples and from existing designs. Even those major seventeenth century military engineers, Coehoorn and Vauban, only added a few new details to the existing systems of defence, without really changing the structural components. Real qualitative progress cannot be demonstrated before the end of the eighteenth or early nineteenth century, when the so-called 'New Prussian ring fortress' with its detached forts came into being. This structurally new type of fortification was not only the result of the unavoidable architectural reaction to highly developed modern artillery with its revolutionary new types of guns and shells. Nor did it evolve only as a result of the appearance of new materials such as steel and later also concrete, used for the construction of a later generation of forts. It also resulted from other new principles of warfare which took into account the longer range of the guns and applied new notions such as spaces under fire-cover and camouflage. The culminating point of this development – being at the same time a step backward – was eventually reached in our own times with the Maginot Line and the Atlantic Wall.

Further Reading

W J Carman, *A History of Firearms from the Earliest Times to 1914* (London 1970).

F E Comparato, *Age of Great Guns: Cannon Kings and Cannoneers who forged the Firepower of Artillery* (Harrisburg 1965).

Christopher Duffy, *Fire and Stone* (Newton Abbot 1975).

Charles Ffoulkes, *The Gun-founders of England* (London 1969).

John R Hale, *Renaissance fortification; art or engineering?* (London 1978).

Ian V Hogg, *A History of Artillery* (London 1974).

Quentin Hughes, *Military Architecture* (London 1974).

Werner Meyer, *Wehrbau Europas* (Frankfurt/Main 1973).

Pierre Rocolle, *2000 ans de fortifications francaises* (Paris 1973).

Volker Schmidtchen, *Bombarden, Befestigungen Buchsmeister* (Dusseldorf 1977).

Eugene-Emmanuel Viollet-Le-Duc, *An Essay on the Military Architecture of the Middle Ages* (Oxford 1860).

Eugene-Emmanuel Viollet-Le-Duc, *Annals of a Fortress*, with a new Introduction by Simon Pepper and Quentin Hughes (London 1983).

ST HELENA, SOUTH ATLANTIC FORTRESS

ST HELENA WAS CONVERTED INTO AN ISLAND FORTRESS BY THE ENGLISH EAST INDIA COMPANY AND BECAME SUFFICIENTLY SECURE TO ACCOMMODATE NAPOLEON BONAPARTE IN HIS FINAL PLACE OF EXILE. **KEN DENHOLM** DESCRIBES THE PROCESS OF FORTIFICATION AND THE SURVIVING REMAINS.

When the Island of St Helena was occupied by the English East India Company in 1659 as a provisioning call for its trading fleet, the first small fort, later called James Fort, was initially the only work considered necessary to defend the island against attack. The Company's view on defence was certainly reinforced by the nature of the island which had a natural barricade of an almost inaccessible surround of high rocky cliffs.

Of other nations who were interested in St Helena, the Dutch had previously claimed it until their attention was diverted to the Cape of Good Hope in 1652. After the English occupation of 1659 they were reminded of its strategic position, and an unsubstantiated account[1] has them capturing it for a short while in 1665 until expelled by the English. But certainly in the Dutch invasion of 1672, the English defences and the massive rocky cliffs did not prove formidable enough, as the Dutch, having landed a force on the western side of the island, went overland to capture the fort which remained in their hands until an English squadron arrived to recapture it during 1673. From that time onwards, St Helena was developed by the East India Company as a fortress in every true sense, not by forts positioned in selected localities, but by fortified lines that sealed off all the possible landing places on the island. Fortunately, the very few landing places were at the narrow sea entrances to deep valleys, and when these were sealed up with fortified lines, the whole of St Helena became a fortress that has never been invaded again.

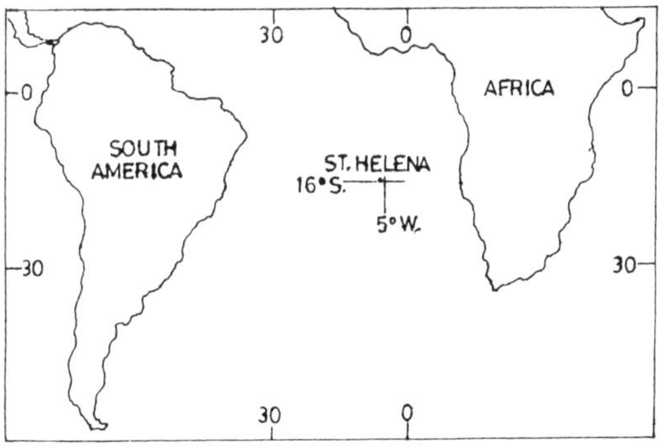

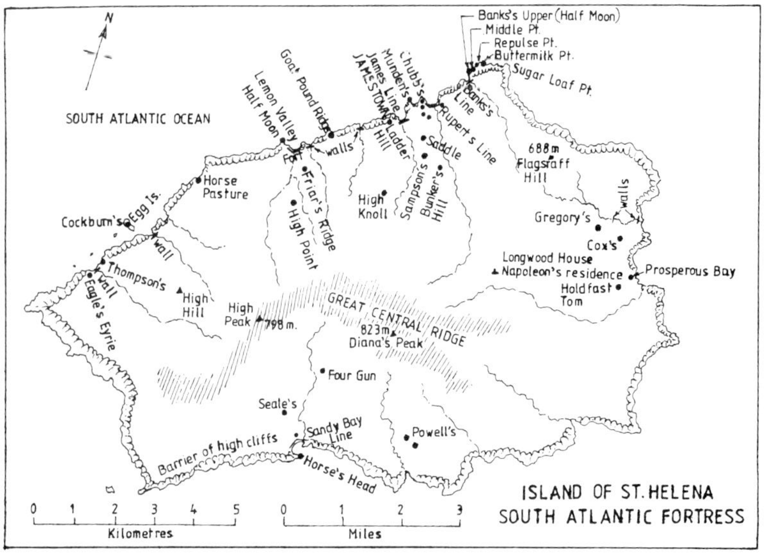

As a prerequisite to creating their fortress, the East India Company established their own military force as a permanent garrison. This was drawn from those who had served with the Company, and was formed into two regiments, the St Helena Artillery Regiment, and the St Helena Infantry Regiment. In the event of another invasion the Company considered that every man on the island would of necessity have to help defend it. Therefore, an additional force, known as the St Helena Militia, was drawn from settlers and their employees. Land grants to settlers were made conditional on their provision of a stipulated number of soldiers per acre, and the resultant Militia force was always available to assist the garrison in the event of an emergency.

THE FORTIFIED LINES

Nearly all the fortified lines on St Helena were built on the north-western or lee side of the island, as that is where nature had provided the few possible landing places at the entrances to respective valleys. But there were a few other valley entrances which were

The Lines, Jamestown 1862. (*John Lilley*)

A recent view of James Line (formerly James Fort 1659) showing curtain walls, moat, and Castle above the terrace. Jacobs Ladder rises on the hillside to Ladder Hill Fort. (*Author*)

so inhospitable that it was only considered necessary to build a wall across the sea entrance without additional fortification. These were referred to in the records as 'walled-up valleys', and the most notable examples to be seen today are at Breakneck Valley, Old Woman's Valley, and Thompson's Valley. Others, of which some ruins can still be seen, are Friar's Valley, Turks Cap Valley, and a valley near Horse's Head.

In addition, from early times there had been a system of stationing outguards on all the strategic high peaks and hills from which any ship approaching the island could be seen at a distance of up to 60 miles, and initially an audible alarm was given by means of gunfire, but this was replaced in 1803 by a much improved telegraph signalling system. Early records show outguards were stationed on Flagstaff Hill, High Peak, High Hill, Sugar Loaf Hill, above Lemon Valley, and at Prosperous Bay.

The development of the fortified lines that basically made St Helena the 'Fortress of the South Atlantic', was a dramatic phase in the island's military history of which very little account has been given. In order of their construction, these were James Line (originally James Fort), Banks's Line, Rupert's Line, Lemon Valley Fort, and Sandy Bay Line.

JAMES LINE

James Bay, where the English East India Company established its first settlement on St Helena, had first been selected as the most suitable landing place by the Portugese who discovered the Island in 1502. It was one of the smaller bays, but being on the lee side of the island it offered a good safe anchorage where ships could take on provisions. The entrance to James Valley lay between two massively steep hills, and it was here, within a stone's throw from the shoreline, that the first fort was built.

Early sketches show the fort to be of triangular shape, consisting of three bastions with the two nearest the sea having seven guns each while the rear bastion had four guns. Two redoubts, one on each side of the fort, each mounted two guns. The fort area was sealed off from the sea by a wall abutting the cliffs at both ends, with the only entrance gate being near to where the wharf gates now stand. In 1673, the fort was supported by Munden's Battery built on high cliffs at nearby Munden's Point.

By 1684, the name of James Fort had been applied and was sometimes called York Fort,

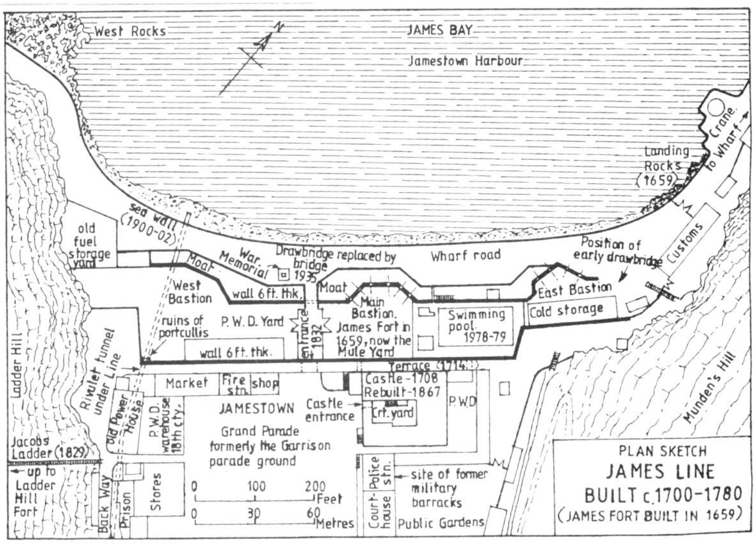

but it was not destined for a long life in its triangular form. After Governor Roberts had the Castle built next to the Fort in 1708, a massive curtain wall that formed a dividing line, and also as a retaining wall for the Castle terrace, was built in 1714. This signified a new strategy in defence that was further emphasised in 1727 when seventy-nine guns were recorded as 'being on the Line'. James Fort was then developed as a fortified line which sealed off entry to James Valley from the sea. In doing so the defenders had to contend with allowing an unhindered flow of the rivulet that runs down the valley, for which a large tunnel had to be formed under the Line, and the relics of a portcullis that was installed in this can still be seen on the curtain wall near the old power house.

In a report for May 1734, the fort was given as defended by two large curtain walls and two 'half-bastions'. The curtain walls can be equated today with those running the full length of the Fort or Line, the outer wall nearest the sea being 6ft (1.8m) thick for gun embrasures, while the inner wall was the dividing line with the Castle as mentioned above. The two half-bastions still exist in a similar form with gun embrasures. Access to the fort was at the eastern end by way of a short moat and drawbridge. In 1977, a Report on Fortifications by Major James Rennell, who had served for a long period with the Company in India, referred to the fort as James Line, mounting thirty-two guns on the Line. A dry ditch or moat which ran the full length of the Line, was completed by 1787.

When Napoleon arrived for captivity in 1815, he had to walk through James Line to gain entry to Jamestown where he stayed just one night. During his period on the island, the fort underwent extensive modi-

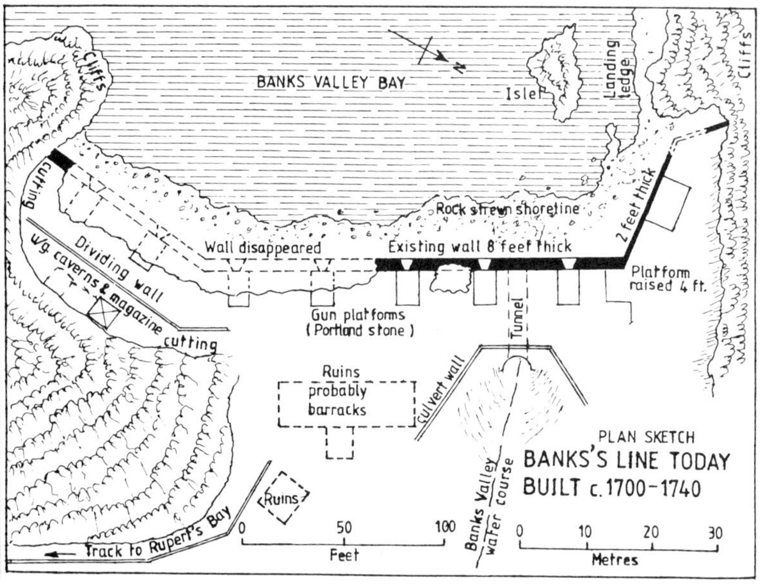

The ruins of Banks's Line across the entrance to Banks Valley (*Author*)

fications including the western bastion which has since been altered, but otherwise James Line as seen today is essentially in the same form. After the Company withdrew and the Island became a Crown Colony in 1834, the garrison was replaced with British Army units, initially the 91st Regiment of Foot in 1836. James Line soon lost its importance as it was considered to be situated too low for effective defence. Thereafter, Ladder Hill Fort on a great hill above James Line and overlooking James Bay, became increasingly more strategic, as also did Munden's Batteries on Munden's Hill.

Extensive alterations to James Line in 1856 were almost certainly more concerned for converting it to civil usage than for military purposes. This was borne out when a tennis court was built by the Royal Engineers on the eastern gun platform in 1889, and a large area of the central platform became a mule yard. But the old guns remained there for a long period, in fact until the Second World War when they were sent to England for melting down as scrap iron. The only guns on James Line today are four old smoothbore cannons mounted at embrasures on the east bastion, and one small cannon on display near the swimming pool, a splendid amenity built by the Royal Engineers in 1978–79. The old moat is now quite picturesque with a grove of large trees and shrubs, while the western end of the Line is presently utilised as plant stores and workshops by the Public Works Department.

BANKS'S LINE

Banks Valley is one of the island's many great carved valleys that run down to the sea where it has a very narrow entrance of only about 80yds (73m) width, but its shoreline was believed by the Company to be suitable as a landing place for an invader, so that gave urgent reason to have it fortified and sealed up.

In 1678, Banks's already had three guns and outguards were stationed there on a day and night rotation system. Its position was vital as ships approaching the anchorage at James Bay, were forced by the south-easterly trade winds to make the manoeuvre of hauling around Sugar Loaf Point and keeping close inshore when passing the entrance to Banks Valley on their way to the anchorage. They would normally have sufficient way to reach the anchorage, but, if too far out, they would be compelled to beat against the wind.

Therefore Banks's was of strategic importance as a fortification to challenge all ships on their approach to James Bay. The Governor had given orders that all ships on reaching a point opposite Banks's, should send in their boat to establish credentials before proceeding. To enforce this process, an additional battery was built 50yds (45m) further out than Banks's; it was called King William's Fort but was actually only a battery. It was later developed quite extensively and known as Banks's Upper Battery (later called Half Moon Battery).

However, at least two large French ships

Banks's Battery 1862–3. (*John Lilley*)

Buttermilk Point Battery: from c1780 the first in line to challenge ships on their approach to the anchorage at James Bay. (*Author*)

Gun crew at Ladder Hill 1862–3. (*John Lilley*)

flying Dutch colours managed to run the gauntlet on 1 June 1706. After responding to the customary warning shot from Banks's battery, they tricked their way past and by sailing on captured two English ships before heading out to sea. Governor Poirier was quite peeved, and reinforced his orders that no ship whatever was to pass Banks's without sending in a boat for permission to land. The reason for the failure of Banks's battery not stopping the French ships was given as insufficient powder and match at hand, while many of the sponges did not fit the guns.

In 1727, when the guns at Banks's had been increased to seven, there was evidence that the fortification to be known as Banks's Line or Platform was in the course of construction. Governor Jenkins was also involved in furthering its progress in 1740. Its final form was mentioned in Major Rennell's report in 1777 when he described Banks's Valley Platform as being 'not more than 80yds (73m) wide and shut up towards the sea by a Battery of 7 guns'. He commended it as being placed with great judgement. To extend the fortifications further along the coast, the Company decided in 1778 to construct a road cut into high cliffs and starting from Banks's. Three batteries built on these cliffs were Repulse Point, Middle Point, and Buttermilk Point, all of which can be seen today along the same road which is now only a rough stony track. Signals from all these fortifications could be relayed to Jamestown via the station on nearby Sugar Loaf Hill and Ladder Hill which was visible about two miles distant.

Banks's Line consisted of a stout curtain wall 8ft (2.4m) thick of stone rubble construction, including seven embrasures and seven Portland stone paved platforms mounting seven guns initially, all set between the narrow valley entrance to seal off access from the sea. A tunnel complete with portcullis, which was formed under the Line to carry storm water, can still be seen today, but sadly no more than one-third of the curtain wall has survived.

A valuable early photograph taken by John Lilley in 1863 showed the fortification intact with seven guns, but it was probably only maintained on a caretaker basis. The same photo showed a long building that must have been the barracks, while a small building with a chimney was probably the cookhouse, but these are now ruins. Several caverns cut into the cliffs served as magazines and a furnace for heating shot. There are ten old guns to be seen today, either lying on the platform or else partly covered by shingle on the shore. All of these are smooth-bore guns about 10ft (3m) long of approximately 6-inch calibre and dated to the early nineteenth century.

From the latter half of the nineteenth century, Banks's Line appears very little, if at all, in the records, and since then the sea has steadily reduced the old curtain wall. The remaining ruins of this interesting early eighteenth century fortified line appear to be awaiting the same fate.

RUPERT'S LINE

After eight guns had been placed at Rupert's Bay in 1678, preliminary work to construct a fortified line across the entrance to Rupert's Valley was begun about the same time as at Banks's. In 1706, it was stated that great endeavours were being made to carry forward the new defensive works at Rupert's Valley which had been begun some time before. The urgency for the completion of this fortified line came from the incident of the same year when Banks's Platform failed to stop two French ships that contrived the capture of two English ships in the Roads at James Bay. But the works were seriously hampered by occasional floods, and, in 1717, were described as so decayed and out of repair that 'a ship could go in there and lie out of reach from every gun'. As the largest bay on this side of the island, it necessitated a curtain

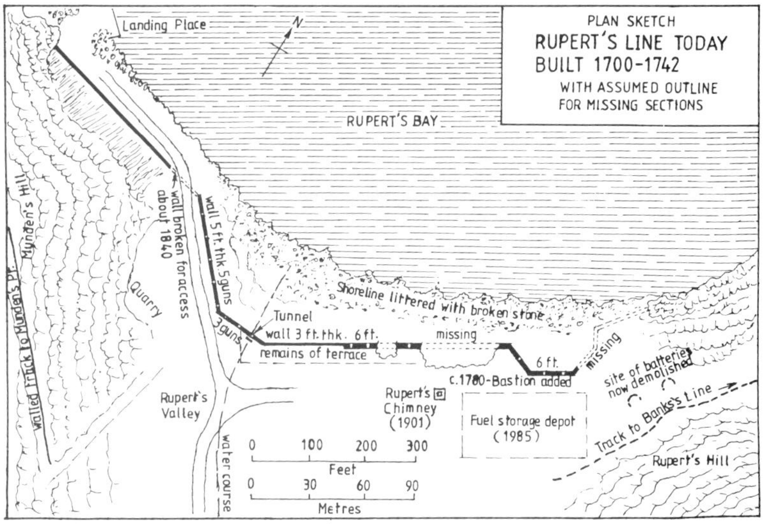

wall of great length, and became a far bigger project than Banks's Line.

In 1742, it was described by Governor Lambert as defective in every respect, further confirmed by Major Rennell in 1777, but his recommendation of flanking batteries was given attention. Several of these were then built on Munden's Hill, including Saddle and Sampson's Batteries. His suggestion for a bastion on the right of Rupert's Line was also

The ruins of Rupert's Line at Rupert's Bay with Munden's Hill in the background (*Author*)

put into effect. In spite of further flood damage, Rupert's Line was restored and was considered to be as effective as the other fortified lines. It mounted up to twenty-one guns. The high curtain wall sealing off the valley, was up to 20ft (6m) high and contained a storm water tunnel with portcullis.

As happened at all the other fortified lines, when the Company withdrew from the island in 1834, and their St Helena Regiments were disbanded, Rupert's Line declined in importance. In 1840, when a depot for liberated African slaves was established at Rupert's Valley, a section of Rupert's Line was removed at its western end to give access to these unfortunate people after they had been brought ashore at the nearby Landing Place, which still exists.

In 1901, when 6000 Boer prisoners of war were held on the island, an ambitious seawater desalination plant was constructed at Rupert's Bay to supply water for the prisoners. This was built alongside Rupert's Line where the high brick chimney with the kilns can still be seen today. A pipeline was built from Rupert's Line to the prisoner of war camp at Deadwood Plain more than two miles away over some tortuous hills. It is believed that the plant was never used except as a trial.

Apart from outguards stationed there during the two World Wars, Rupert's Line has served no further military purpose. However, Rupert's Bay has advanced in importance with the establishment, during the 1980s, of a storage depot for fuel and oil which is pumped ashore from a tanker that anchors in the Bay. The new power station was built further up the valley in 1985. This century, Rupert's Line has suffered great damage from the sea and today there is no more than half the original curtain wall remaining. Unfortunately, this interesting example of the defensive system that established St Helena as a fortress, seems to be doomed unless a scheme of preservation can save it.

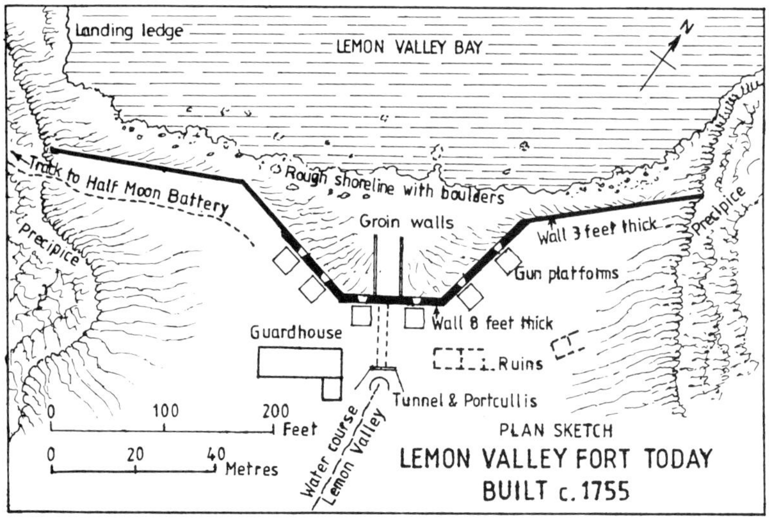

LEMON VALLEY FORT

On the western side of the Island, Lemon Valley is more spectacular and scenic than all the others. This great deep cleavage winds its way down to be joined by Sarah's Valley and meets the sea at Lemon Valley Bay. Here, between sheer high cliffs on both sides, the Dutch landed in 1672, but were foiled by English defenders throwing down showers of boulders from the precipices. The Dutch retreated and sailed off to make a successful landing believed to have been at Bennet's Point further along the coast, from where they went overland and captured the Fort.

After the English recaptured the island in 1673 they knew only too well that Lemon Valley Bay was a suitable landing place for an invasion. Until something more positive could be done to fortify it, they stationed outguards on a full-time basis. By June 1678, the locality just a short distance from the landing place at Lemon Valley Bay was fortified with five guns and became known as Sprague's (but soon changed to Bearkley's) Platform.

From Company records of 24 September 1707 their Engineer, John Newman, gave approval for improvements to the defences which were then referred to as Lemon Valley Fort. A guardhouse, magazine, and platform on the eastern side with three guns, and another on the western side with two guns, were all built on the high ground of small hills to be clear of floods. At this time the only personnel afforded for Lemon Valley Fort was one officer and two soldiers. By 1717, these works were described as ruins with the gun platforms having been broken for the past six years. In the same year, the locality just up the valley from the fort was used to quarantine victims of smallpox which had broken out amongst slaves who had been brought from Madagascar. At that time Lemon Valley Bay was used as a common watering place for ships as there was a very good spring up the valley.

In 1734, the old guns at Lemon Valley Fort were so flamed and honeycombed they were all taken away and placed on the West Rocks of Jamestown Harbour where one of them can be seen to this day with the muzzle embedded into the rock. In 1742, Governor Lambert stated that Lemon Valley was a

place of great dangers and the fort insufficient to stop an enemy. In his suggestion for a breastwork to be linked with the hills on either side to seal up access to the valley, he was advocating the same strategy practiced elsewhere on St Helena. But for a long time no attention was given to his advice, and during October 1753 a great flood washed away the guardhouse which was supposed to be clear of floods.

Shortly after this catastrophe, work commenced on the construction of the curtain wall sealing off the valley from the sea and making Lemon Valley Fort a fortified line. It was a massive project by any standards, and the present splendid condition of this fortification is a tribute to those who built it; that is slaves, labourers, stonemasons, engineers, and prisoners who were compelled to work a period on the fortifications as part of their punishment. In spite of being in a very remote area, Lemon Valley Fort today is in a better condition than all the other fortified lines with the exception of James Line.

The curtain wall stretches unbroken for 200yds (180m) to join the precipices at both ends, but for those who visit it today a portion at the southern end has been removed to allow access to the shore and the landing place. Alternatively, one may go through the storm-water tunnel where a portcullis once existed. Averaging a height of about 20ft (6m) and up to 30ft (9m) at the northern end, the wall contains a recessed section 9ft (2.7m) thick at the centre for six gun embrasures with Portland stone sills. The paving slabs for the gun platforms are also of Portland stone. An old guardhouse in fair condition and the ruins of several smaller buildings are nearby.

The report by Major Rennell in 1777 described this fort as being closed up by a fortified line of a better construction than any of the others. Outlying redoubts for the fort suggested by him were later added: Half Moon Battery, Friar's Ridge Battery, and High Point Battery. The St Helena regiments manned the fort, but the 20th Foot Regiment of the British Army were stationed there for a period in 1819 during Napoleon's captivity.

When the East Indian Company withdrew from St Helena in 1834, Lemon Valley Fort still had six 9-pounder long guns and three 18-pounder carronades, but there are no guns today, although its redoubt, Friar's Ridge Battery, has a good carronade. The locality was used as a depot for liberated African slaves who were landed there from 1840 and were accommodated further up the valley, where many ruins can be seen today. The ruins of a quarantine station exist nearer the fort.

To reach Lemon Valley overland has always been a very arduous, even dangerous journey, but quite recently the track down the valley was greatly improved for easier access to this fascinating old fortified line. It

Half Moon Battery, 1862–63. (*John Lilley*)

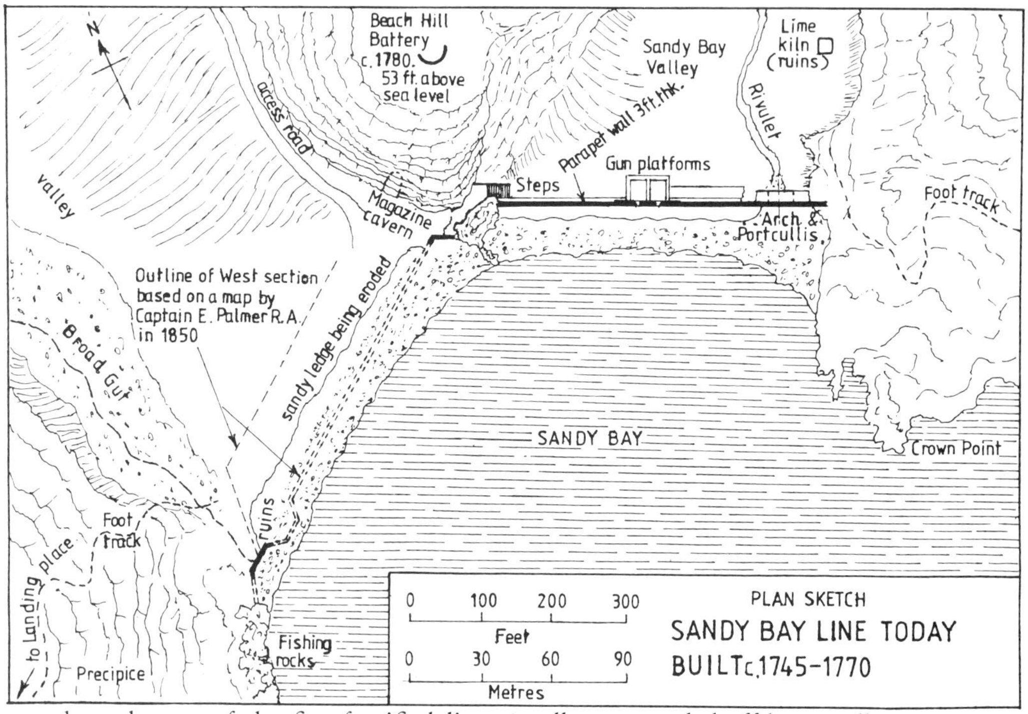

was the only one of the five fortified lines that was usually referred to as a fort. Judging by the sound condition of its curtain wall, there is no threat to its survival.

SANDY BAY LINE

The wide stretch of very rough shingle forming the inner Sandy Bay shoreline is directly exposed to the prevailing south-easterly wind which all too frequently whips the bay into a frenzy of raging sea. Nevertheless the Company believed an invasion might be attempted there. The first reference to Sandy Bay was on 28 November 1695 when orders were given by the Company to build a battery for two guns. In 1734, when the battery had four guns, all these and their carriages were washed away in a storm and it was acknowledged that the battery had been built too near the sea.

In 1742, Governor Lambert was on hand to give advice as he had done so often for other fortifications. He proposed a platform of guns on both the east and west ends of the Line. More significantly, his further proposal was to join the right- and lefthand platforms with a drystone wall, into a continuous Line, which is exactly the form that was soon adopted at Sandy Bay Valley and Broad Gut Valley. But his decision to build the wall without using mortar in order to expedite the work, was a bad mistake that condemned the wall to a short life. The western section was smashed down by the sea a long time ago.

An extensive walled-up landing place was built opposite Horse's Head on the south-west side of the bay, while a small nearby valley was sealed off by a wall to prevent an enemy landing and going over the steep hills to reach the rear of Sandy Bay Line. The combined length of the east and west sections of Sandy Bay Line was no less than 400yds (370m), making it a project of monumental proportions and the longest fortified line on St Helena. The main walls as evidenced from the existing eastern section were nearly 3ft (1m) thick but increased to 4ft (1.2m) where gun embrasures were positioned. The height of the wall was up to 20ft (6m).

Today it can be seen that all the western half of Sandy Bay Line has disappeared leaving a fragile sandy ledge which is being consumed by the sea at an alarming rate. A conglomeration of ruins below Beach Hill give way to the intact eastern wall which includes the gun platform where the two old long guns and two carronades are lying in a terribly corroded condition. Their platform is formed from massive granite slabs 6in (15cm) thick that might be the only granite ever imported to St Helena. At the extreme eastern end of the Line, the wall is arched over the Sandy Bay rivulet, and although some restoration work has been done here, there is dangerous loose masonry above.

By the latter half of the nineteenth century Sandy Bay Line had been placed on a caretaker basis, and for well over one hundred years it has not been used for military purposes, although outguards were stationed there during the World Wars. Sandy Bay is today a recreational locality, especially for rock fishing, but unless some urgent remedial work is undertaken, the valuable old military

Sandy Bay Line east section, with gun platforms and arch over rivulet

relic of Sandy Bay Line cannot survive in its present shaky form.

Affiliated batteries that were built in support of Sandy Bay Line include Horse's Head Battery, Seale's Battery, and Four Gun Battery, while Beach Hill Battery on a rise above the Line, could be considered to form part of it.

FORTRESS FOR NAPOLEON'S CAPTIVITY 1815–1821

In addition to the fortified lines and walled-up valleys, the East India Company had attended to the defences in practically every remote corner of the island, where many small batteries were situated. These included such positions as Turks Cap, Prosperous Bay, Powell's Valley, Thompson's Valley, Ladder Hill, and Munden's Hill.

By now in effect the island was a fortress, and that certainly prompted the British authorities to select it for Napoleon's captivity from where there was no chance of him escaping. To reinforce this, the Royal Navy established St Helena as a naval station with patrols maintained by five brigs circling the island day and night, while of five warships stationed at Jamestown Harbour, two were always cruising.

As a further precaution, a new battery was established on Egg Island, the largest of the offshore islands. It was named Cockburn's Battery after Rear-Admiral Sir George Cockburn (initially in supreme command on St Helena), and armed with carronades and three guns of 6-inch bore [32-pounders?]. The latter can still be seen today. The St Helena Regiments were greatly reinforced by British Army units, namely the 53rd Regiment, 66th Regiment, 20th Regiment, Royal Artillery, and Royal Engineers.

The walled entrance to Old Woman's Valley as part of the East India Company defence strategy, *c*1780. (*Author*)

DEFENCE STRATEGY AFTER CROWN RULE

After the Company's rule officially ended in 1834, the era of St Helena being a fortress also ended, because the preservation of the island was assured by the supremacy of the Royal Navy which, from 1840, was very active in the region on anti-slavery patrols. With the declining value of the old fortified lines and batteries, for a long period St Helena figured very little if at all in new defence strategy, although the garrison was maintained by British Army units and the St Helena Militia continued to exist on a volunteer basis.

The next development was the building in 1886 of two new batteries on Munden's Hill for RML (rifled muzzle-loading) guns which had been developed since 1860. These two guns of 9-inch (23cm) calibre and more than 12 tons in weight, arrived from England in June 1888. They can be seen today lying on the ground near the batteries that later replaced them. Ladder Hill Fort was upgraded about the same time with similar new batteries, but the most spectacular addition was the rebuilding of the High Knoll Fort which had existed since 1790.

At this time there was an active phase of fort construction being carried out in England, and High Knoll Fort in its strategic position at 2000ft (620m) above sea level, incorporated the most advanced military design. The construction work, begun by the Royal Engineers in 1874, was completed about 1894. As the only inland fort on the island, its purpose was twofold: firstly for its guns to bear on James Valley and Ladder Hill should an enemy break through either of those coastal defences; secondly, it was also

clearly intended to serve if necessary in siege conditions. It had a very large, strongly walled, perimeter within which all the island residents could be accommodated during any invasion. This fort is today a significant military relic. Probably its most vital duty was to serve for incarcerating the more dangerous amongst the 6000 Boer prisoners of war who were held on St Helena during 1900–1902.

Early twentieth century defence strategy focused on protecting Jamestown Harbour for which both Ladder Hill Fort and Munden's Hill Batteries were essential. New 6-inch BL pedestal-mounted guns for two new batteries on Munden's Hill and at Lad-

der Hill Fort were maintained by the Royal Marines who formed the garrison on St Helena from 1911 until 1939. The two 6-inch naval guns installed in new batteries at Ladder Hill were not new guns; they had been previously mounted on Royal Navy battleships. They were manned from 1939 to 1945 by the Royal Artillery, and can be seen today, complete with armoured shields mounted on their batteries, which were fed ammunition by chain conveyors from underground magazines. Other military relics that can be seen at Munden's Point, are the searchlight positions constructed during the Second World War. These were manned by the Royal Engineers and the St Helena Rifles, which was a local unit raised on the Island.

Since 1946 St Helena has not been garrisoned and nor does it have any militia force as a standby, but spread around this little island there remains a fascinating array of military relics that, in its heyday, made it the 'Fortress of the South Atlantic'.

Footnote:
1. Mentioned in 1897 by Frederick Danvers in his *Introduction to the List of Factory Records of the East India Company.*

Ladder Hill Artillery Barracks 1852. (*John Lilley*)

THE 'GIBRALTAR OF THE WEST INDIES': BRIMSTONE HILL, ST KITTS

VICTOR T C SMITH DESCRIBES THE HISTORICAL DEVELOPMENT OF THIS REMARKABLE CARIBBEAN FORTRESS AND EXPLAINS THE PHILOSOPHY BEHIND THE CURRENT PROGRAMME OF CONSERVATION, HOW IT IS ORGANISED AND PRESENTED TO THE GROWING NUMBER OF TOURISTS TO ST KITTS.

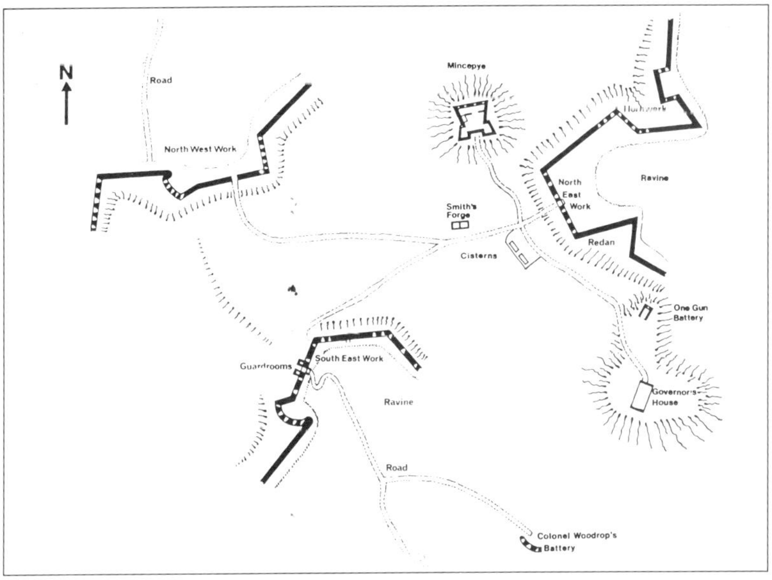

Brimstone Hill Fortress, 1723

On top of a small coastal mountain on the island of St Kitts in the eastern Caribbean is the dramatically situated and monumental Brimstone Hill Fortress. The name of the fortress is said to derive from the sulphurous odour which is released from a volcanic centre in the sea bed a short distance from the nearby shore. From modest and tentative beginnings in the 1690s, the site developed into one of the most powerful English fortresses in the Caribbean. It covered 40 acres (16.2 hectares) and was built on three levels, from the lowest at 550ft (168m) to the highest at 780ft (238m). By the early nineteenth century, it came to be known as the 'Gibraltar of the West Indies', not only because of its great strength, but because when viewed from the south, the Hill looked a little like Gibraltar. Brimstone Hill saw action against the French on three occasions: in 1690, 1782 when the fortress was besieged for a month, and in 1806.

Abandoned in 1853 following British defence cuts in the West Indies, the site returned to nature to be rapidly overgrown with bush and trees which obscured from view the gradually decaying buildings of the fortress. Around the end of the nineteenth century, the historical consciousness of the government of St Kitts was stirred and it began to make an allocation of money to maintain some of the buildings, to clear bush and to make the site accessible to visitors. From then on, in the ensuing decades of the twentieth century emerged a veritable time capsule: an entire fortress of the eighteenth century and Napoleonic Wars, unaltered by later development, forming the remains of a complete mountain-top military community which, in effect, is what it had been.

Fort George with its caponiers and two places of arms. In the top right of the photograph is Fort Charles, the need for whose rear protection gave rise to the Brimstone Hill Fortress. (HMS Invincible, *1986*)

Through a sustained programme of repair, restoration and re-armament from the 1930s, the fortress has become a successful visitor monument administered since 1985 by the Brimstone Hill Fortress National Park Society (formerly from 1965 the Society for the Restoration of Brimstone Hill). For the last several decades, this activity has been led by Mr Lloyd Matheson, CBE, and it is largely to his efforts that the good progress made is due.

This exciting site possesses some interesting and even unique features and must be regarded as an internationally important military monument. Yet, it is not widely known by historians or more generally outside the region. One of the intentions of this article is to promote a wider awareness of the Brimstone Hill fortress and of its current and future programme of restoration and presentation to the visitor.

THE RATIONALE AND DEVELOPMENT OF THE FORTRESS

The design and function of the fortress evolved over a period of time. It began in 1690 as a temporary artillery fire position to help drive out the French who had captured the English Fort Charles on the shore line about 500yds (457m) from the Hill. This fire position on the Hill was then made permanent to support Fort Charles in the event of further attacks by the French. The latter had, by treaty, gained possession of the southern and northern ends of the island since 1627, with the English colony sandwiched between. This arrangement was a source of strife and difficulties until, confirmed by the Treaty of Utrecht in 1713, the whole of the island passed to the English.

After 1690, Brimstone Hill began to be seen as a convenient place for a 'Deodand', or retreat for the occupants of the island in the event of invasion – exclusively seaborne following the end of French title to St Kitts. It was used for this purpose certainly as early as 1706. In the several ensuing decades of the eighteenth century the hilltop was, under the supervision of the Lieutenant Governor William Matthew, protected by a discontinuous bastioned trace. A plan of 1723 (in the collection of the Duke of Buccleuch) showing the work of Matthew indicates that the walls were designed to block the way against infiltration up the several ravines which existed, into the body of the place. The northernmost of two small twin peaks on the hill was occupied by a citadel known as the

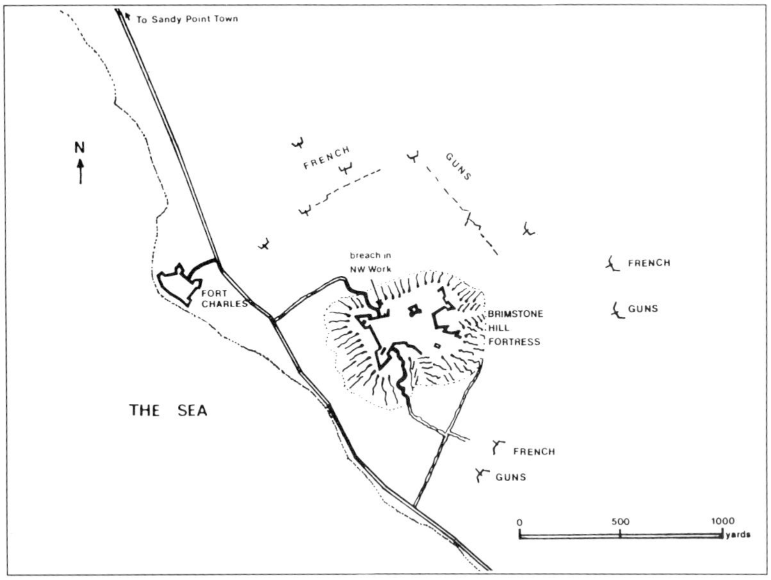

Greatly simplified plan of the French gun positions at the siege of Brimstone Hill in 1792

'Mince Pye', because of its shape when viewed from the side; the southern peak was surmounted by the governor's house. Aside from the battery in the left face of the North-West Work to support Fort Charles and several north-facing gun positions on the Mince Pye, the fire plan of the fortress gun embrasures was, in the main, for close-in defence of the near approaches and the heads of the several ravines. It was not primarily conceived to defend against a regular siege and would have needed guns in different positions to achieve that object. In 1734, there were 41 cannon at the fortress. These were of various sizes and in varying condition.

Warfare in the islands was usually triggered by, and was an extension of, conflict in Europe between the powers. This led to direct action by naval and military forces against each other's Caribbean territory. Between wars in Europe, an uneasy peace was maintained. In 1778 France joined with the insurgent American colonies, declared war against England and warfare in the Caribbean ensued. Later, taking advantage of his country's naval superiority in the waters around the island, the French General, Marquis de Bouille invaded St Kitts on 11-12 January 1782. He was able to land an army of 8000 men and invested the fortress within a few days. Realising that the rest of the island would be captured by the French, about 1000 British troops and island militia had taken refuge in the fortress to defend it and hence retain title to the island. Although extemporised batteries were built by the defenders to try to cope with the French siege batteries which surrounded the fortress, the original conception of the position to resist infiltration attack by the ravines only, did not help its power of resistance. Nevertheless, the defenders held out for a month and finally succumbed to surrender when two large breaches were opened in the walls of the North-West Work, from French gun positions which it had been difficult for the guns of the fortress to silence. By then the supplies of the fortress had been almost exhausted and few cannon remained serviceable. The heroic resistance against overwhelming odds without any possibility of outside succour impressed the French who, after the surrender, allowed the garrison the honour of marching out with their drums beating and flags flying.

Lessons had been learnt from the insufficiencies of the design of the fortress during the siege and within a few years of the return of the island to the British following the Treaty of Versailles in 1783, a major and expensive reconstruction of the defences of Brimstone Hill was begun. This was to lead to the 'Golden Age' of the fortress.

The fundamental tactical difference which this process brought about was the adaptation of the fortress to resist a regular siege from long-range breaching batteries. This was achieved by means of the provision of prepared emplacements aligned to fire on those places on which an enemy might be expected to place his bombardment batteries in a siege. In addition, new positions were established both to support Fort Charles from the rear and to fire at long range on the anchorage at Sandy Point. How all this was accomplished was through the construction of new and powerful artillery fire positions. These were:

(a) the Prince of Wales Bastion just below the northernmost of the twin summits of the hill;
(b) a Citadel and outworks to replace the earlier Mince Pye, collectively known as Fort George; and
(c) further emplacements on the southernmost summit – or Monkey Hill as it was called – around the governor's house. Some gun positions were also provided in the older discontinuous bastioned lines which were repaired and in some places raised in height.

Fort George is of particular historical interest and importance. Designed in 1789 and substantially completed by the mid-1790s, it is a fully developed caponiered polygonal fort of very early date. It contains the division of offensive and defensive weapons between the ramparts and caponiers which was

The North-West Work with successive tiers of fortifications rising behind. *(D L Matheson)*

the characteristic of the polygonal system. The barracks and magazines were in casemates under the ramparts.

The remarkable increase in the number of guns to be served and the need to accommodate an adequate force of infantry against assault required a very considerable increase in barrack establishment. For officers, a long and imposing barrack for the Infantry was constructed at the side of the flattened Parade area between the twin summits with, nearby, a most imposing and handsome quarters for the officers of the Artillery. Engineer and other officers were accommodated in build-

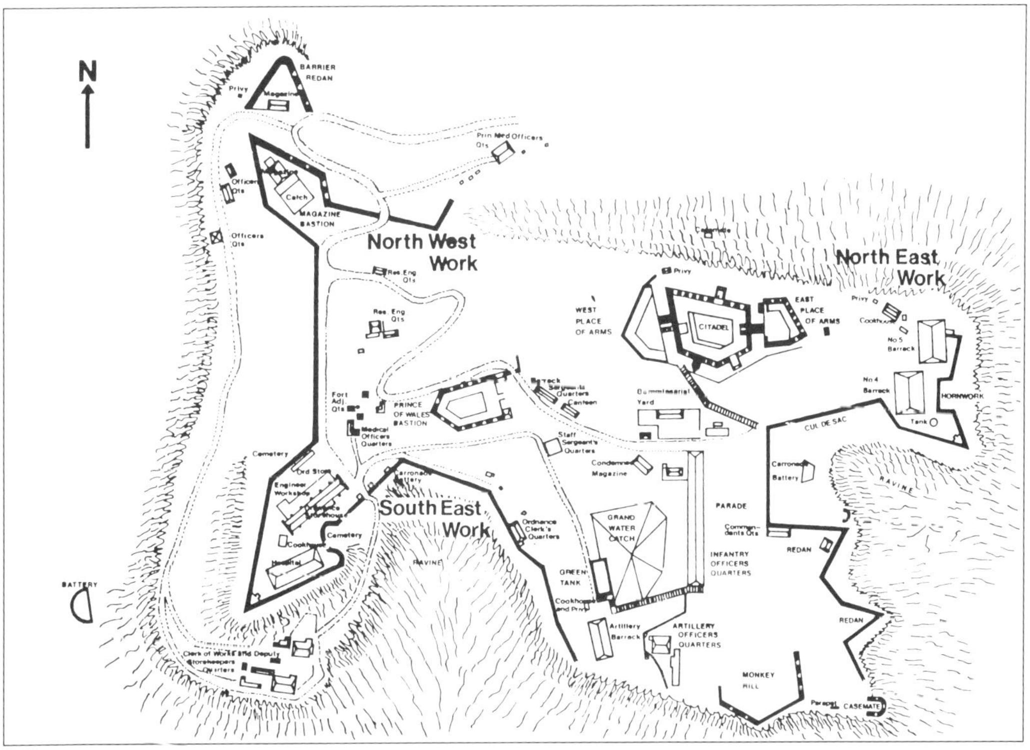

Brimstone Hill Fortress, 1810

ings elsewhere in the fortress. Other ranks were accommodated within Fort George, in a barrack below the latter within the old North-East Work and in other places. There were, by the Napoleonic Wars, so many buildings on the Hill that it assumed the appearance of a small mountain-top town.

Water supply to the fortress was entirely from the rains. Below the Infantry Officers' quarters was a large water catchment which emptied into storage tanks having a capacity of 100,000 gallons (455,000 litres). Other major storage tanks existed within Fort George and the older North-West and South-East Works. There were also numerous small water butts fed from the roofs of individual buildings.

The fortress last saw action in 1806 when its guns reportedly drove off a force of French ships under Prince Jerome Bonaparte which was advancing against British shipping moored off Sandy Point.

After reaching its zenith in the Napoleonic Wars, the primacy of Britain in the Caribbean somewhat reduced the necessity of maintaining such a large and powerful fortress. Further, a contemporary document states that the need to defend the Sandy Point anchorage had ceased to be a matter of importance since few vessels now moored there. By the later 1820s it was proposed to reduce its large number of mainly unserviceable guns (78 in 1828) to 27 serviceable ones. Little action seems to have been taken however. One of the reports on the armament dated 1829 does however throw an interesting light on the tactical expectation of the fortress: guns of Fort George and its outworks were expected to fight at ranges of 2000–3000yds (1800–2750m) over land and sea which meant that they would be firing to the very limits of their effective range.

The days of the fortress were numbered and apart from various necessary repairs and refurbishments carried out in the 1840s it seems to have been held at little more than a care and maintenance level. In 1853, Britain withdrew her military establishments from St Kitts, Dominica, St Vincent and Tobago, and the Brimstone Hill fortress was abandoned.

RESTORATION AND PRESENTATION TO THE VISITOR

The fortress is managed by the Brimstone Hill Fortress National Park Society for the St Kitts Government, which owns the site. There is a General Manager (who is accountable to the Society's Council of Management), a Park Manager, a Museum

Custodian, a shop assistant and a group of groundsmen. The Society is empowered to make regulations for the protection of the National Park. These are at present being drafted and will be enacted in due course as legislation of the St Kitts Government.

The extensive works of stabilisation, repair and restoration which have been undertaken over the years have been, and will continue to be, expensive. Grants from donor bodies are vital to enable this work to continue. In past years, the fortress has benefited from grants by the British Development Division, the Caribbean Conservation Association, the Canadian International Development Agency, the Organisation of American States, the Government of St Kitts, and others. These grants have been for specific repair and restoration projects. Much of the actual works has tended to be undertaken by local contract labour and, in its own way, this has helped to keep alive some of the local stonemasonry

The right flank of the Western Place of Arms of Fort George, with the Dutch island of St Eustatius in the background. (*D L Matheson*)

The interior of Fort George. (*D L Matheson*)

The north face of Fort George. In the siege of 1782, the fortress was bombarded by the French from the lower slopes of the mountains in the background. (*Victor T C Smith*)

skills. It is hoped to form a Conservation Corps from local volunteers to undertake various conservation tasks.

Day-to-day running costs are found by the Society itself which has to finance itself through entrance fees from visitors to the fortress, subscriptions and merchandising. The National Park Society has to be financially effficient in order to survive. This important site is going to need all the help it can get from donor agencies in the years to come if it is to take its rightful place in the international historical heritage community.

Maintaining the grounds of the fortress is particularly demanding, especially with the steep slopes of the site. The combination of sun and plentiful rain encourages grass and bush to grow at a remarkable speed when compared with historic sites in the United Kingdom and in much of Europe. Four or five groundsmen (usually in short supply during the cane-cutting season), as well as a variety of motor mowers, strimmers, chainsaws and growth-inhibiting sprays, are employed six days a week all year round in an effort to keep the growth under control. In some places, exposed parts of the fortress would return to nature in less than a year if not judiciously kept trimmed.

The restoration and presentation of the fortress to the visitor offers both enormous possibilities as well as great challenges. The emphasis to date has been upon the repair, rebuilding and stabilisation of structures as well as the creation of a museum within Fort George. This has also been supplemented by the mounting of some 42 cannon (mainly 18-pounders and 24-pounders) behind most of the extant embrasures of the fortress. The visual impact of these cannon is striking. The next stage in the evolution of the fortress as a heritage monument is to make it 'live' for the visitor through reinstatement of selected areas to original appearance and by the use of modern interpretation techniques by which the rationale and development of the fortress may be effectively communicated in an interesting and lively way. This will be effected by the projection of strong visual images of how the fortress used to be. The problem and the objective is to present a multi-structure organism of:

(i) the guns, material and the fighting role of the fortress;
(ii) the men, their families and their lives and deaths; and
(iii) the fortress organisation and infrastructure and how it related to the wider community around it.

The process of constructing the fortress, its architecture, the role of slaves in the building

Brimstone Hill from the south. (*Victor T C Smith*)

The magazine of Magazine Bastion (eighteenth century) with successive tiers of fortifications behind. (*Victor T C Smith*)

Caponier on the south face of Fort George. (*Victor T C Smith*)

process and the siege of 1782, will be among a range of themes to be developed in a series of exhibitions and displays. Deciding upon how to go about presenting the fortress is one issue; settling upon where within the fortress to do this is another. Because the fortress is on several levels there are considerable vertical distances between those levels. This means that presentational aspects have to be matched to the realities and practicalities of visitor movement, access and management. For the foreseeable future, practical considerations will mean that the vast majority of visitors, almost all of whom enter the fortress by motor vehicle, will have to unload on the Parade on the upper level which is the only practicable turning and parking area. Added to this, the greatest concentration of interesting and visible structures, the largest single visitable area and the finest views of the country, the sea and the fortress are to be found within easiest reach from the Parade area. This includes Fort George, Monkey Hill and the Prince of Wales Bastion. It is therefore at this level where most effort will be concentrated.

A start upon the implementation of a major presentational strategy has already been made in the form of the restoration and re-building of the Commissariat building on the edge of the Parade as a Visitor and Orientation Centre and an enlarged merchandising facility as well as in the restoration, and re-furnishing of the Warrant Officers' Quarters, to present the human factor.

During 1990 will begin an evocative presentation of the Prince of Wales Bastion as a fire position. The structure has already been stabilised and it is fully armed. Pyramids of reproduction shot are to be displayed on the *terre-pleins*, together with side-arms, and replica portable magazines. The stone-built magazine for the bastion will be fitted out as it had been in the Napoleonic period, with powder barrels and will have a suitably dressed mannequin in a work pose. The guardroom will also be reinstated. Broadly the same treatment will be given to Fort George, but with the addition of a reinstated barrack room and bake-house both having appropriately dressed and posed mannequins. These activities are merely the start of a longer-term strategy to bring to life the whole of the fortress by a series of reinstate-

Fort George from the Infantry Officers' Barracks. (*Victor T C Smith*)

ments. Plans are also being made to introduce up to twenty specially designed interpretation panels at key places within the fortress. These will each provide the visitor with a view of the area of the fortress as it would have been seen from behind the panel in the eighteenth century or Napoleonic period. The panels will also include other informative drawings and information.

It is intended to provide a range of tour options, so that the visitor may spend as little as half an hour or as much as a half-day or more enjoyably and informatively touring the various features of the fortress. This will

Inscribed stone in an embrasure of the East Caponier of Fort George: 'Georg Wale – 3 Buff – 1798'. (*Victor T C Smith*)

Facade of the soldiers' barracks in the North-East Work. (*Victor T C Smith*)

The restored and rebuilt Warrant Officers' Quarters. (*Victor T C Smith*)

include the availability of both short and long trails, with interpretative leaflets to go with them.

Restored forts and fortresses have a strong potential educational value for schools and colleges. The production of a teachers' handbook has therefore been initiated as part of a policy which not only aims to make the fortress more relevant to historical and environmental studies of schools in St Kitts but will, over a period of time, encourage more and more Kittitians to regard the fortress as part of their heritage. This will also be fostered by steps being taken to develop greater community use of the fortress.

The possibility of encouraging suitable schemes of private investment is also to be considered. These will typically be projects which will exchange a concession for undertaking business activity on the site for an agreement to repair and reinstate the buildings and areas selected for that activity. This will need careful handling to ensure that the visual integrity of the fortress is maintained but does hold out the prospect of a means of achieving a more extensive and rapid scheme of restoration than would otherwise be the case.

A start will be made on the archaeological investigation of any parts of the fortress subject to erosion loss (particularly on the edges of hill slopes). The area around the Commissariat building is to be excavated and recorded prior to the completion of the Visitor Centre project. For the longer term, there is a large amount of research archaeology to be undertaken in unthreatened areas to answer specific historical or architectural questions. An archaeological research centre within the fortress will be needed as a consequence.

The Brimstone Hill Fortress has a crucial part to play in the tourism development of St Kitts and is one of the foremost tourist destinations on the island. It is expected that it will have an ever increasing role in further improving tourism prospects. There are certainly exciting and developmental years ahead for the Brimstone Hill Fortress. The

Mr J Bass, a master mason repairing a quoin stone of the Commissariat Building. *(Victor T C Smith)*

Three phases of stonework in the North-West Work from the early eighteenth century until the Napoleonic period. *(Victor T C Smith)*

The main rainwater catch adjacent to the Parade of the fortress. (*Victor T C Smith*)

Colonnade of the basement of the Infantry Officers' Quarters. (*Victor T C Smith*)

aim is to make it the foremost interpreted defence heritage site in the Caribbean, to which the visitor will come to experience a fortress as a complete military community – 'people as well as guns'.

An application has been made for inclusion of the Brimstone Hill Fortress in the UNESCO World Heritage List. Its historical and architectural importance, especially with the significance of its early polygonal citadel, make the fortress a natural selection for listing. The Brimstone Hill Fortress National Park Society hope that their application will be successful.

The Brimstone Hill Fortress is one of a range of important fortifications in the Caribbean whose defence heritage sites demand more attention from historians. The idea that Caribbean fortifications were a small collection of minor works, chiefly against pirates, is untenable. The West Indies became a battleground for the European powers from the later sixteenth century. This is reflected in a large number of fortifications, some of considerable size, built by the English, French, Spanish, Dutch, Danes and by the Americans which deserve special study and assessment for the rich interest which they present.

Editor's Note

The history and development of the Brimstone Hill Fortress is to be the subject of a paper in a future issue of *Post Medieval Archaeology* and a note on Fort George will appear in *Fort*, the journal of the Fortress Study Group.

GUANTANAMO BAY'S ARMY FORTIFICATIONS, 1898–1917

DALE E FLOYD DESCRIBES THE CONSTRUCTION BY THE US ARMY OF THE LITTLE-KNOWN BATTERIES IN GUANTANAMO BAY, CUBA.

The 1898 Spanish-American War added new territories including Puerto Rico and the Philippines, to the already large expanses of the United States. The country renounced title to Cuba from the beginning, although many citizens championed its annexation, hoping to indicate that the war was not fought to acquire more territory but to give the people in that island a chance to determine their own destiny. The United States did, however, realize Cuba's strategic position and quickly negotiated a hundred-year lease to parcels of land at Guantanamo Bay for a naval base.[1]

Since the American Revolution, the Army, among its many duties, had constructed defences for the Navy's dockyards and bases as well as the country's major ports and harbours. Thus, after dispatching various delegations of military personnel, including George Dewey and George W Goethals, to Guantanamo Bay to study the terrain and

Fort McCalla, looking north-west

Edward H Schultz

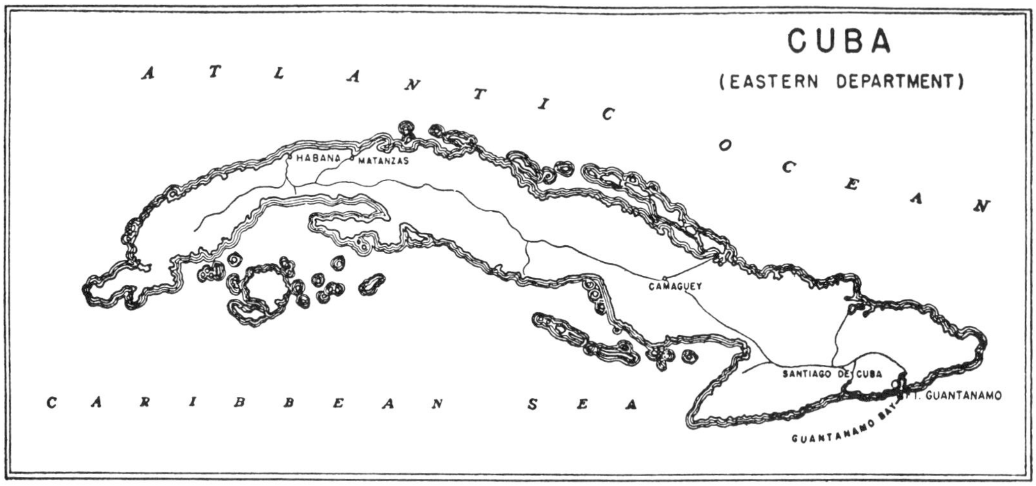

determine the defensive requirements, the Army began planning for the new naval base's defence. These efforts coincided with the deliberations of the Taft Board, a commission composed of military and civilians and chaired by William Howard Taft, whose mission was to formulate plans for the defence of the United States and its territories.[2]

The Taft Board decided that Guantanamo Bay was one of eleven highest priority ports that required defences. It determined that the base needed six 12-inch guns, four 3-inch guns, and eight mortars with a total estimated cost for guns, carriages, and emplacements of $1,504,800. In addition, the Board estimated $125,046 for submarine mine defence, $114,000 for searchlights, $280,606 for fire-control, $103,727 for a central power plant, and $43,076 for a reserve power plant. The total estimated cost for the defence of Guantanamo Bay was $2,171,255.[3]

In the meantime, Congress appropriated $250,000 for use during the 1906 fiscal year to construct defences at Guantanamo Bay. Actually, the Government allotted $20,000 on 6 February 1905 for the submarine mine defences, $180,000 on 22 March 1905 and $12,000 on 27 April 1907 for the gun batteries, and $5000 on 27 January 1906 for an ice plant. Except for some other paltry sums, this $217,000 constituted the only allotted funds for the Guantanamo Bay defences. Although Congress did consider the Taft Board recommendations, it failed to provide the suggested funds for Guantanamo.[4]

In the spring of 1905, the War Department dispatched Engineer officer Captain Edward H Schulz to Guantanamo Bay to begin preparations for the construction of the defences. He determined where to erect the various structures, hired labourers, purchased the required building materials, and began construction. The work included the submarine mine defences, an ice plant, a battery for four Model 1905 6-inch guns on Model 1905 disappearing carriages west of the entrance to the Bay at Conde Bluff, and a battery for four Model 1903 3-inch rapid-fire guns on Model 1903 pedestal mounts to the east at Fisherman's Point.[5]

Fort Conde

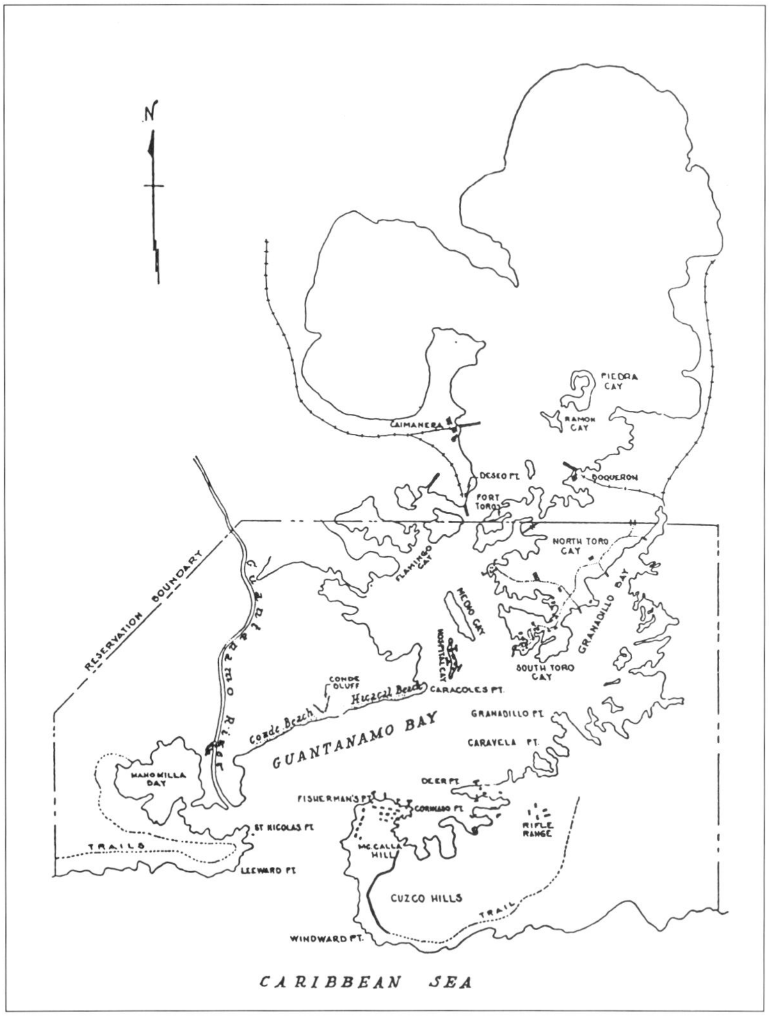

US Naval Station, Guantanamo Bay, Cuba, 1908

By the end of fiscal year 1906, the completed submarine defence structures comprised a mining casemate, a torpedo storehouse, a cable tank, a loading room, and two fire-control stations, one primary and one secondary. In fiscal year 1907, construction of a magazine began and the labourers completed the installation of the electric wiring.[6]

Schulz laid all the concrete for the battery, two works about 276ft (83m) apart, each with two 3-inch gun emplacements, later collectively termed Fort McCalla, at Fisherman's Point and completed one-half of the earth parapets in fiscal year 1906. The next fiscal year, he finished the parapets and placed the iron doors, grating and telephone booths. In July 1907, the Chief of Ordnance suggested that the Army send the four 3-inch rapid-fire guns and their pedestal mounts, intended for Guantanamo Bay, to the Philippines, which expected but did not experience, a Japanese invasion. Although, the guns and mounts did not apparently go to the Philippines, they never arrived at Guantanamo Bay either – at least, not while Army personnel were still there.[7]

Lieutenant Warren T Hannum, who succeeded Schulz on 20 May 1907, oversaw some of the construction of the 6-inch gun battery, often referred to as Fort Conde, at Conde Bluff. By the end of fiscal year 1907,

Fort McCalla, South 3-inch battery. (*National Archives photograph 77-F-114-190-15, June 1906*)

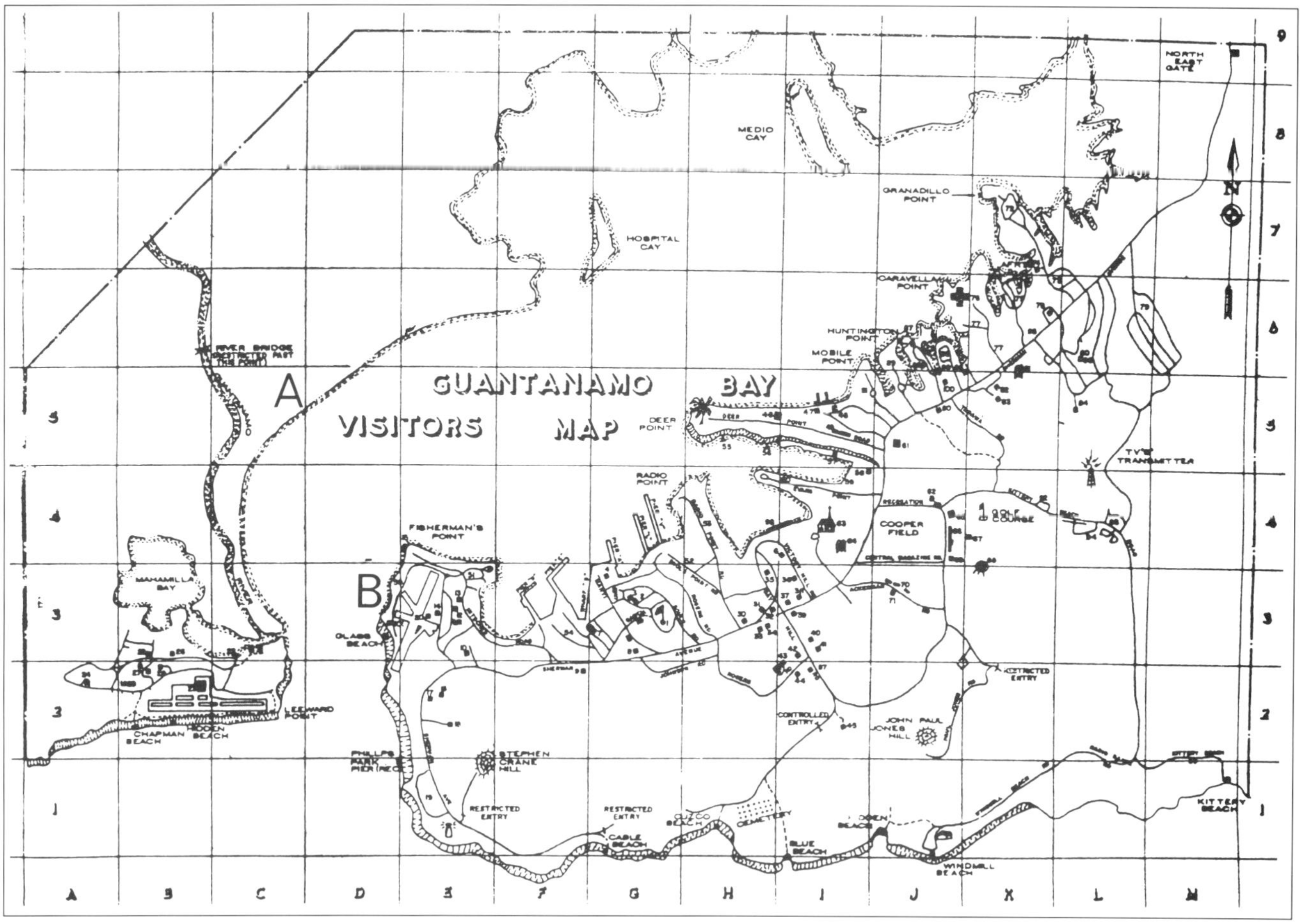

Guantanamo Bay Visitors Map ('A' = Fort Conde, 'B' = Fort McCalla)

Fort McCalla, 3-inch battery, right flank, emplacement No 1. (*National Archives photograph 77-F-114-187-4, June 1908*)

Warren T Hannum

Fort Conde, 6-inch disappearing carriage, M1905, No 3, mounted in No 3 emplacement. (*National Archives photograph 77-F-114-187-7-14, 1908*)

the battery still required the completion of three-quarters of its earth parapet, installation of the electric wiring, and the mounting of the carriages and guns. Soon afterwards, Hannum mounted the disappearing carriages.[8]

Other engineer construction at Guantanamo Bay included four sets of living quarters, one office, one mess hall, one windmill, and one ice plant at Fisherman's Point and a power house for the battery at Conde Bluff. The labourers also laid 7500ft (2133m) of narrow-gauge railroad track and installed a 30-inch searchlight, purchased by the Navy, at Conde Bluff. When the Army left Guantanamo due to lack of funds for further construction, the Navy and Marine Corps received custody of all this property. In spite of contemporary and subsequent plans, this construction comprised the total Army defence construction at Guantanamo except for some minor work during wartime.[9]

In the years following this construction, the Army and Navy continued to stress the

Casemate, cable tank, loading room and storehouse as completed, all pertaining to Torpedo Building. (*National Archives, March 1907*)

Fort Conde, M1905 disappearing carriage, No 5, mounted in emplacement No 1. (*National Archives photograph 77-F-114-187-7-12*)

Fort McCalla, (portable) searchlight shelter in the rear of and between the 3-inch battery. (*National Archives photograph 77-F-114-187-7-6b 1908*)

need for additional fortifications at Guantanamo. In April 1913, the Chief of Engineers submitted an estimate of $2,155,000 for fortification construction at Guantanamo to include four 14-inch low level batteries, two 4-gun mortar batteries, two 6-inch batteries of two guns each, and one 3-inch battery of two guns. This proposal, like others, failed.[10]

Congress had not officially approved the development of a naval base at Guantanamo Bay and, therefore, the Appropriations Committee refused to consider estimates for fortifications at that place.[11] Thus, in reply to an inquiry from the Secretary of the Navy, the Secretary of War stated, in September of 1916:

> . . . I beg leave to inform you that the completion of the defensive plans for Guantanamo, including the selection of the exact sites for sea-coast batteries, has been deferred by the War Department, pending further development of that locality as a naval base; and that information as to the exact sites of these batteries will be communicated to the Navy Department as soon as a decision in the matter shall have been reached.[12]

Since their construction, the Guantanamo Bay army defences have stood, unprotected from the elements, as reminders of the army role in naval base protection. They still stand today, generally unknown.[13]

Notes

1. No 46285/12, General Correspondence, 1894–1923, Record Group 77, The Records of the Office of the Chief of Engineers, National Archives Building (hereafter referred to as RG-77).

2. Bradley Michael Reynolds, 'Guantanamo Bay, Cuba: The History of an American Naval Base and Its Relationship to the Formulation of the United States Foreign Policy and Military Strategy Toward the Carribean, 1895–1910', PhD dissertation, University of Southern California, 1982, pp279–80 & 311; George Dewey to Secretary of the Navy, 11 October 1904, No 110451, General Correspondence, 1897–1915, Record Group 80, General Records of the Department of the Navy, National Archives Building (hereafter referred to as RG-80); Robert S Browning, *Two If By Sea: The Development of American Coastal Defense Policy* (Westport: CT) 1983, pp30, 143–44, 159, 186–88; No 46285 & 16, General Correspondence, 1894–1923, RG-77; Dale E Floyd, *United States Coast Defense, 1775–1950: A Bibliography* (Washington, DC 1985), page xxix; B D Varner and Daniel Koze, *The History of Guantanamo Bay*, Third Edition (Guantanamo Bay, Cuba 1964), p11.

3. US, National Coast Defense Board, *Report of the National Coast Defense Board . . . on the Coast Defenses of the United States and the Insular Possessions, Senate Document No 248*, 59th Congress, 1st Session (Washington, DC 1906), pp24 & 26; No 54140/346, General Correspondence, 1894–1923, RG-77.

4. US, Congress, House of Representatives, *Seacoast Batteries at Guantanamo Bay, Cuba: Letter from the Secretary of the Treasury, Transmitting a Copy of a Communication from the Secretary of War Submitting an Estimate of Appropriation for Batteries at Guantanamo Bay, Cuba, Document No 260*, 59th Congress, 1st Session (Washington, DC 1905), p2; Money Statement to Accompany Annual Report for FY 1907, filed with Annual Report for Defenses of Guantanamo Bay, Cuba, for the Fiscal Year Ending 30 June 1907, No 64324, General Correspondence, 1894–1923, RG-77.

5. Annual Report for Defenses of Guantanamo Bay, Cuba, for the Fiscal Year Ending 30 June 1905, pp1–3, No 56113/2; Annual Report for Defenses of Guantanamo Bay, Cuba, for the Fiscal Year Ending 30 June 1906, p1, No 56113/6, No 46285/63–64, 91, 95, 114, 116, 134, 142–444, 162, 170, 172, 203–04; General Correspondence, 1894–1923, RG-77; Varner and Koze, *The History*, pp11 & 25.

6. Annual Report for Defenses of Guantanamo Bay, Cuba, for the Fiscal Year Ending 30 June 1906, pp1–2, No 56113/6; No 46285/169, 333, 410; General Correspondence, 1894–1923, RG-77.

7. Annual Report for Defenses of Guatanamo Bay, Cuba, for the Fiscal Year Ending 30 June 1906, pp2–4, No 56113/6; Annual Report for Defenses of Guantanamo Bay, Cuba, for the Fiscal Year Ending 30 June 1907, pp1–2, No 64324; No 46285/312, 333, 383, 410, & 442; General Correspondence, 1894–1923, RG-77.

8. No 6513/3; Annual Report for the Defenses of Guantanamo Bay, Cuba, for the Fiscal Year Ending 30 June 1907, pp1–2, No 64324; No 46285/436; General Correspondence, 1894–1923, RG-77.

9. Annual Report for the Defenses of Guatanamo Bay, Cuba, for the Fiscal Year Ending 30 June 1907, pp2–4, No 64324; No 46285/410, 495, 500, 540, 572, 582, 588, 603, & 656; General Correspondence, 1894–1923, RG-77; No 1286710 filed with No 962281, Document File, 1890–1917, Record Group 94, Records of the Adjutant General's Office, 1780s–1917, National Archives Building (hereafter referred to as RG-94); No 11045/166 & 407, General Correspondence, 1897–1915, RG-80.

10. No 69298, General Correspondence, 1894–1923; 'Guantanamo', page Memoranda – 1, Coast Defense Fortification File, 1898–1920; RG-77; No 1440491/A filed with No 962281, Document File, 1890–1917, RG-94.

11. No 1440491/A filed with No 962281, pp1–2, Document File, 1890–1917, RG-94.

12. No 2435127-A filed with No 962281, Document File, 1890–1917, RG-94.

13. Varner and Koze, *The History*, p 25.

Acknowledgements

I wish to thank Brigadier-General Edwin H Simmons, USMC (Ret), Director of Marine Corps History and Museums, and Captain William R Solms, USN, for providing recent aerial photographs of Fort McCalla and Fort Conde.

THE CAREW CASTLE PROJECT 1986–1990

SANDY GERRARD REPORTS ON THE SIGNIFICANT FINDINGS OF ARCHAEOLOGICAL WORK RECENTLY CARRIED OUT ON BEHALF OF THE PEMBROKESHIRE COAST NATIONAL PARK.

The familiar view of Carew's Tudor face, from the other side of the mill pond. (*Beaufort*)

Carew Castle, (SN 045037) in the old Welsh county of Pembrokeshire (now Dyfed) is probably best known for its very fine late Tudor extension complete with a range of impressive mullioned windows overlooking the still waters of a nearby mill pond. In any study of castle architecture Carew generally appears towards the end of the story and highlights the shift from defence towards the residential. Carew's history is however, much more complex. The site was first inhabited during the Iron Age when a five-ditched promontory fort was constructed. Occupation of the site continued into the Roman period and Dark Ages. When the Normans arrived they erected a castle within the existing fort. As time passed, the castle was extended to take in much of the area now known as the Castle Green. By Tudor times, the wealth and influence of the owners was reflected in the architectural splendour of the castle and some of the smaller medieval rooms were replaced by spacious apartments. In the early part of the seventeenth century the castle was the scene of several skirmishes, and, at the end of the Civil War, the southern side of the building was slighted. From this time on the fabric deteriorated and took on the form of romantic ruin and environmental oasis.

THE ARCHAEOLOGICAL PROJECT

In 1984, the Pembrokeshire Coast National Park leased the castle and its immediate environs from the Carew Estate, with the aim of conserving the unique ruins, improving their setting and increasing public access and

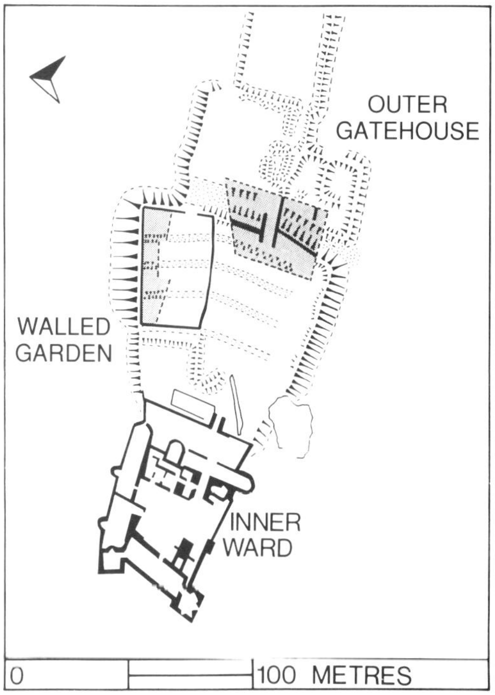

General plan showing the location of the excavation areas, the upstanding castle and promontory fort

enjoyment. It was soon appreciated that a large-scale archaeological excavation would greatly enhance the monument's appeal, by providing new information and uncovering further structures. In the short term, it was felt that the excavation itself would be an important attraction, with visitors to the site encouraged to watch work in progress, share in the discoveries and learn about the processes of excavation.

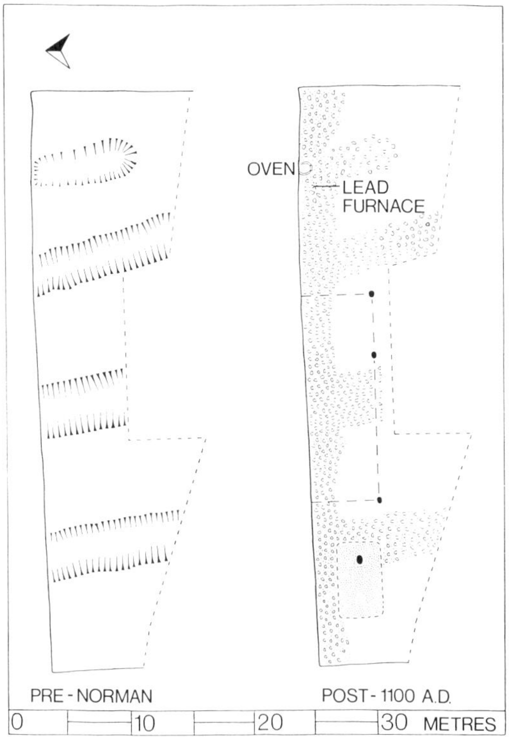

Simplified plan of Walled Garden excavation area

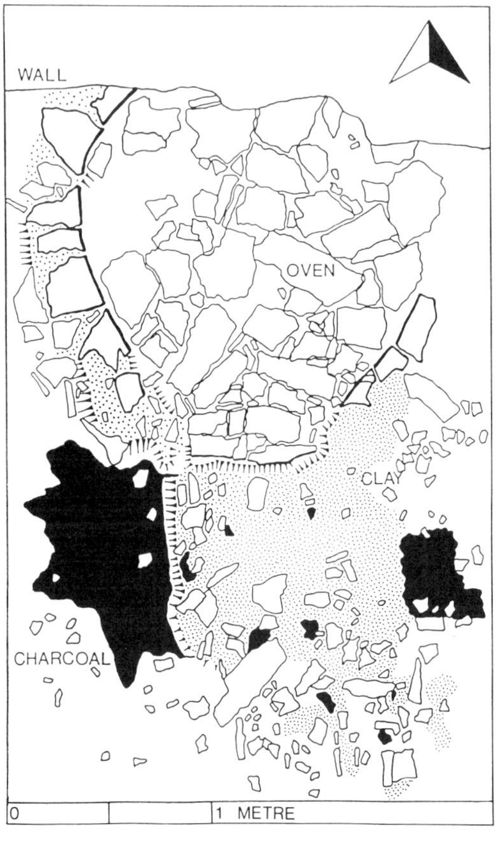

Plan of Norman bread oven

Between 1986 and 1990, several areas of the castle were investigated, including parts of the Lesser and Greater Undercrofts, the South-West and Chapel Towers. Most effort has been directed at the Outer Ward where excavations in the Walled Garden and Outer Gatehouse area have provided important information concerning the site's character and development. This review deals only with this aspect of our work.

THE WALLED GARDEN

The Walled Garden at Carew occupies the north-eastern corner of the medieval Outer Ward. Its northern and eastern walls are primarily medieval curtain wall. Excavations in the garden were carried out in advance of the anticipated construction of an Interpretation Centre for the castle. Removal of the garden soil rapidly revealed that the majority of post-thirteenth century levels had been destroyed, though encouragingly, some had survived. The most significant features included a seventeenth century lead furnace, and the very ephemeral remains of a small sixteenth century rectangular building.

Documentary and architectural evidence indicates that the Outer Ward was constructed under the direction of Sir Nicholas de Carew towards the end of the thirteenth century (Cathcart King, 1962, Figure 1). This was confirmed archaeologically.

The limestone bedrock slopes down towards the north, and, to compensate for this, the builders had to level up the northern area. In addition, earlier hollows had been backfilled to provide a level platform. The material used contained considerable quantities of twelfth and early thirteenth century artefacts. Foremost amongst these were sherds of Ham Green (near Bristol) cooking pots and jugs and various Barnstaple wares. Metalwork (including arrowheads, knives, nails, keys, studs, forks and sheeting), animal bones, shells and worked stone, including a complete millstone, were all recovered. These artefacts must represent refuse from the earliest Norman occupation of the site, and it is interesting to note their use in a land fill operation similar to that of modern times. Evidence for structures associated with the platform was slight. No occupation surfaces survived, but three post holes cut into the bedrock may relate to a rectangular building, butted up against the northern curtain wall.

At one point, a relatively well-preserved stone oven was found below the thirteenth century platform. This structure was oval in shape and its door faced south. This oven had been buried when the platform was constructed and a silver penny of King Stephen (*c*1140) was found amongst the ashes raked from its last firing. It may represent the early Norman bakehouse at Carew, and its position, some 95m (312ft) downwind from the Norman castle could be explained as an early fire prevention measure. Much of the original castle may have been timber, and ovens were notorious fire hazards.

IRON AGE PROMONTORY FORT

The most significant features found below the thirteenth century platform were five parallel rock-cut ditches. Their maximum depth was 2.00m (6½ft), and although their upper fill contained Norman artefacts, their lower fill held only animal bones, fragments of a shale bracelet and large quantities of snails. The five ditches were cut across the width of the rocky promontory (their position can be traced in the form of cropmarks). They would have had a stone and earth rampart set on their western edge. Behind these defences a settlement can be anticipated, although the precise character of this has not yet been determined. The existing castle probably covers the area originally occupied.

Dating of the fort continues to be a problem. The evidence is, a date of 220 ± 80 ad (HAR-8994) from animal bone in the primary silt of one ditch and a number of Roman sherds and a possibly contemporary bronze brooch from the secondary fill of another. This would suggest that at least one of the rock-cut defensive ditches was Iron Age whilst the other may be Romano-British. The similarity of the fill deposits lends support to the current hypothesis that the ditches are approximately contemporary, and that the defences therefore consisted of five separate ditches and ramparts. Further evidence for early occupation of the site was provided by the recovery of a large amount of Roman pottery (some 300 sherds), tiles, glass and metalwork, though the focus of this settlement remains to be found. In addition, a small number of seventh century imported 'E ware', sherds were found suggesting continuity of occupation.

The discovery of a previously unknown Iron Age promontory fort, Romano-British and Dark Age settlement at Carew has emphasized the importance of the site.

THE OUTER GATEHOUSE AREA

Excavations within the area known as the Outer Gatehouse commenced in August 1987. During the medieval period, this area was the site of the Outer Gatehouse, parts of the Outer Ward buildings, a moat and a series of quarries. Excavation has revealed a complicated sequence of events finishing with large scale stone robbing.

The absence of any meaningful stratigraphy over large parts of the Outer Ward (the turf and topsoil rests directly on the bedrock in many places) meant that the few surviving surfaces are incomplete and disconnected. Enough of the original curtain wall and gatehouse survive to indicate the character of the ground plan. The curtain wall is surprisingly wide at 3.4m (11ft), and built of very small limestone blocks. Only short lengths of the medieval gatehouse walling survived, although clearly defined robber trenches made it possible to establish the ground-plan (dark shading). Traces of the medieval road leading to the castle were uncovered both to the east and west of the gatehouse. It was, however, impossible to ascertain the full character of this road and the moat bridge, since the decision to consolidate the remains at the overlying Tudor road surface precluded further examination. Par-

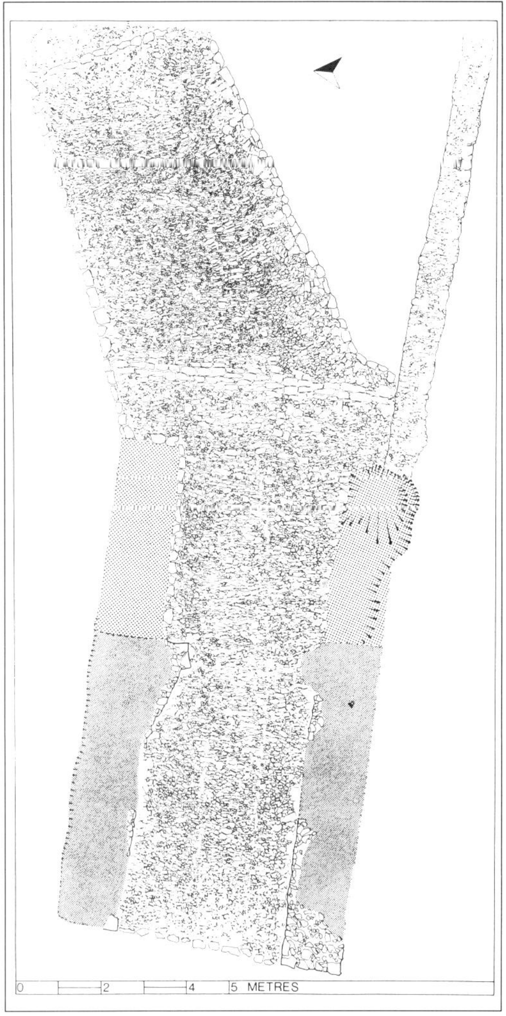

Plan of Outer Gatehouse area

Plan of Medieval and Tudor Outer Gatehouse showing surviving walls and robber trenches with cobbled road

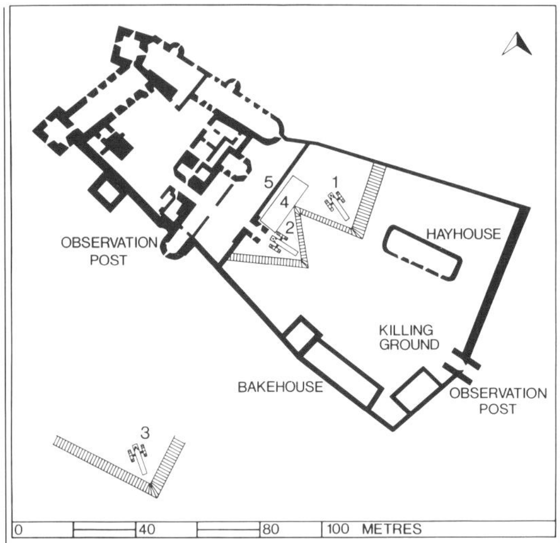

Civil War Carew

tially underlying the medieval surface and extending southwards, was a series of small quarries. These had been backfilled with thirteeth century material including a number of fine arrowheads, knives and other metalwork. A more substantial quarry measuring 1.9m (6½ft) deep and partially cutting the filling of an Iron-Age rock-cut ditch was found within the Outer Ward. These quarries were probably dug to provide stone for the first period of construction at the castle.

During the medieval period, a rock-cut moat extended the entire length of the eastern side of the Outer Ward. Excavation of the moat revealed a ditch which attained a depth of up to 3m (10ft) and preliminary ceramic analysis indicates that the majority of the silts accumulated before the middle of the fourteenth century, and by 1500 the ditch would have ceased to provide an effective barrier against even the most ill-equipped attacker. The distribution of finds indicate that large quantities of rubbish were thrown from the bridge leading from the gatehouse and across the moat. The moat, in its surviving form, seems to have been medieval, though it is probably on the line of an earlier promontory fort ditch.

A large number of lengths of wall uncovered seem to be associated with the documented Tudor expansion of the castle. In the south-east corner, the walls and paving of a small formal garden were found. The more substantial wall built immediately south of the cobbled roadway may have been a low boundary designed to prevent vehicles straying off the main thoroughfare. The slender wall on the top of the slope leading up from the moat is certainly of Tudor date, but the plan would suggest that it closely follows the line of the earlier curtain wall.

Considerable quantities of Tudor pottery were recovered along with a very fine lead badge with a swan motif and a silver groat of Elizabeth I.

The medieval gatehouse was considerably extended in the Tudor period (figure opposite in the lighter shading). This situation is paralleled at the castle's Middle Gatehouse where a Tudor extension of precisely the same dimensions at ground level is attributed to the work for Sir Rhys Ap Thomas and dated to around 1500 (Cathcart King, 1962, p278). Two separate cobbled surfaces leading westwards through the gatehouse were found. The uppermost of these (*c*1590) was of a rough character and it was not possible to define its edges clearly. Below this lay an extremely well preserved and finely constructed cobbled roadway, defined at its edges by a substantial stone kerb. This earlier surface is confined to the gatehouse passage and the area immediately above the earlier moat, with the roadway at either end being less clearly defined. Its surface is reminiscent of the abraded cobbled surface within the castle's Inner Gatehouse. Throughout the length of the gatehouse, two parallel ruts denoting the use of wheeled transport are clearly visible and in the area immediately above the backfilled moat, where the road surface has sunk slightly, a crude open drain was laid to carry surface water through the retaining wall into the vestiges of the moat. At one point, three Tudor post-holes had been cut into the medieval road surface. Their location suggested that they might represent flag poles or some similar form of decorative feature.

Finally, it is believed that the deflection of the road towards the north on passing from the gatehouse is attributable, not to any de-

Medieval moat north of the Tudor roadway. View from the north

fensive consideration, but rather in order to avoid a substantial building (whose earth covered ruins still survive) immediately to the east of the excavated area.

THE ARCHAEOLOGY OF THE CIVIL WAR

The major consequences of the Civil War on the architecture and archaeology of Carew have traditionally been seen as the destruction of the Kitchen Tower, the southern Inner Ward wall, the levelling of the entire Outer Ward, the construction of a ravelin outside the Middle Gatehouse and a number of small alterations to the fabric of the castle to benefit the use of muskets. Recent excavation and fieldwork have indicated that this picture needs to be revised. It is uncertain whether the demolition of the Kitchen Tower wall was due to artillery or mining. The latter seems the more likely given the extortionate costs and effort of bringing down such a substantial wall with cannon alone.

Traditionally, it has been argued that the entire Outer Ward was levelled in order to provide a field of fire for artillery positioned within the ravelin in front of the Middle Gatehouse (*eg* Cathcart King, 1962, p276). There are, however, a number of problems with this interpretation. First, a hayhouse described as standing in 1592 (PRO Exch T of R Misc, Book No 151) still partially survives to this day. There is no reason why this building alone should have survived, particularly as its position is more likely to have adversely affected the efficiency of the castle's artillery more than any other structure. Second, the Buck print of 1740 clearly shows that at least part of the Outer Ward wall was standing at this relatively recent date. Third, preliminary mortar analysis has indicated that a large part of the northern wall of the Walled Garden is medieval. This confirms that large lengths of the medieval Outer Curtain survive, and this would certainly support the idea that the Outer Ward formed an integral part of the castle's defences during the Civil War. Fourth, the earliest map of the castle [1751] shows only a small section of the eastern outer wall missing, and, more significantly, a roofless building is shown standing on the site of the Tudor bakehouse. Finally, a copper token found below the rubble from the destruction of the outer curtain wall has been dated to about 1660. Clearly, this stretch of wall is extremely unlikely to have been knocked down before 1660. It now seems most likely that the defence of Carew took the following form. Three artillery batteries were con-

View of Tudor road and gatehouse. View from the east

structed, two immediately outside the Middle Ward [1 & 2] and the third in the field to the south [3]. The position of Nos 1 and 2 suggest that they could have been used for two purposes. First, at long range, they could have fired at the approaching enemy with the aid of an observation post situated on top of the Outer Gatehouse. Secondly, at short range, if the Outer Gatehouse was stormed the artillery in each battery would have provided cross-fire on the area immediately inside of the Outer Gatehouse, turning this part of the castle into a killing ground. The important point here is that it would not have been necessary to demolish the outer walls to provide a field of fire, since this could be better achieved with a forward and elevated observation post. In addition, it would seem to make little sense to remove a perfectly adequate defence line, remembering that parts of the wall were over 3m (10ft) thick.

The third artillery emplacement [3] would have provided protection for the southern aspect of the castle and, perhaps more importantly, would have allowed the garrison to control the highway between the church (where a second garrison was stationed) and the castle. Observers for this post may have been situated within the south-east tower.

The substantial stone-lined pit [4] situated immediately outside the Middle Gatehouse has been interpreted as many things, including cesspit, horse-dip and moat, but it would now seem to fit more comfortably within a Civil War context. Situated immediately behind two artillery batteries it is possible that it was a magazine, where gunpowder in particular was stored immediately prior to being taken to the nearby guns. The advantages of such a position are obvious, because, if the magazine received a direct hit the damage would be minimized by the surrounding ground taking the force of the explosion. If the gunpowder was stored above ground an explosion could have demolished large parts of the castle, killing many of the garrison. The defenders would have appreciated the special need to protect their largest source of gunpowder, and to this end the large number of musket loops [5] placed in the wall immediately above this area may provide support for this interpretation. There is a significant absence of loops on the other side of the gatehouse.

On the basis of the existing evidence it seems likely that the Outer Ward was utilized during the war and therefore, the widespread robbing which it has clearly suffered must be more recent. Dating the destruction is difficult, but a possible context would be the lime-burning carried out in the latter part of the eighteenth century at a lime-kiln situated just to the south of the Inner Ward (Sandby print of 1779).

Excavations at Carew have been suspended whilst post-excavation work and consolidation are carried out, but work will recommence in 1992, when it is hoped there will be an opportunity to examine the inner wards.

Further reading

D J Cathcart King and J Clifford Perks, 'Carew Castle, Pembrokeshire', *The Archaeological Journal* CXIX (1962), pp270–307.

ELLA ARMITAGE, CASTLE STUDIES PIONEER

JOAN COUNIHAN EXAMINES THE GROWTH OF CASTELLOLOGY IN ENGLAND AND THE BACKGROUND TO ELLA ARMITAGE'S CLASSIC BOOK *EARLY NORMAN CASTLES*.

Between 1905 and 1911 Mrs Ella Armitage (1841–1931) wrote a series of long and interesting letters to Harold Sands, FSA, about the work both she and he were doing in the field of earthworks and early Norman castles at that time. He had been kept busy excavating at Hastings and at Pevensey, Sussex, while she had been equally busy in Yorkshire preparing material to go into the *Victoria County History* for that region, which was later published in 1912. She had a Mr D H Montgomerie, FSA working with her – drawing the diagrams to match her text. He was the link, it appears, which brought Ella Armitage and Sands together, Montgomerie having worked also with Sands on his earlier digs. A significant letter from her, dated 24 January 1907, marks, to my mind, the foundation of castle studies and castle study groups as we know them today. But possibly my statement may be as much open to controversy as many made by the early participants in the battle of words which took place at the beginning of the century about the origins of Norman castles in England.

In this letter she wrote – in reply to his written just before Christmas 1906 –

> I think there was never a truer word written on this subject [castles] than what you say in your letter, 'We shall never do any good till we have a book of the chronology of castles based on record testimony that will be accepted as beyond argument.' I have some ideas on the subject which I hope to communi-

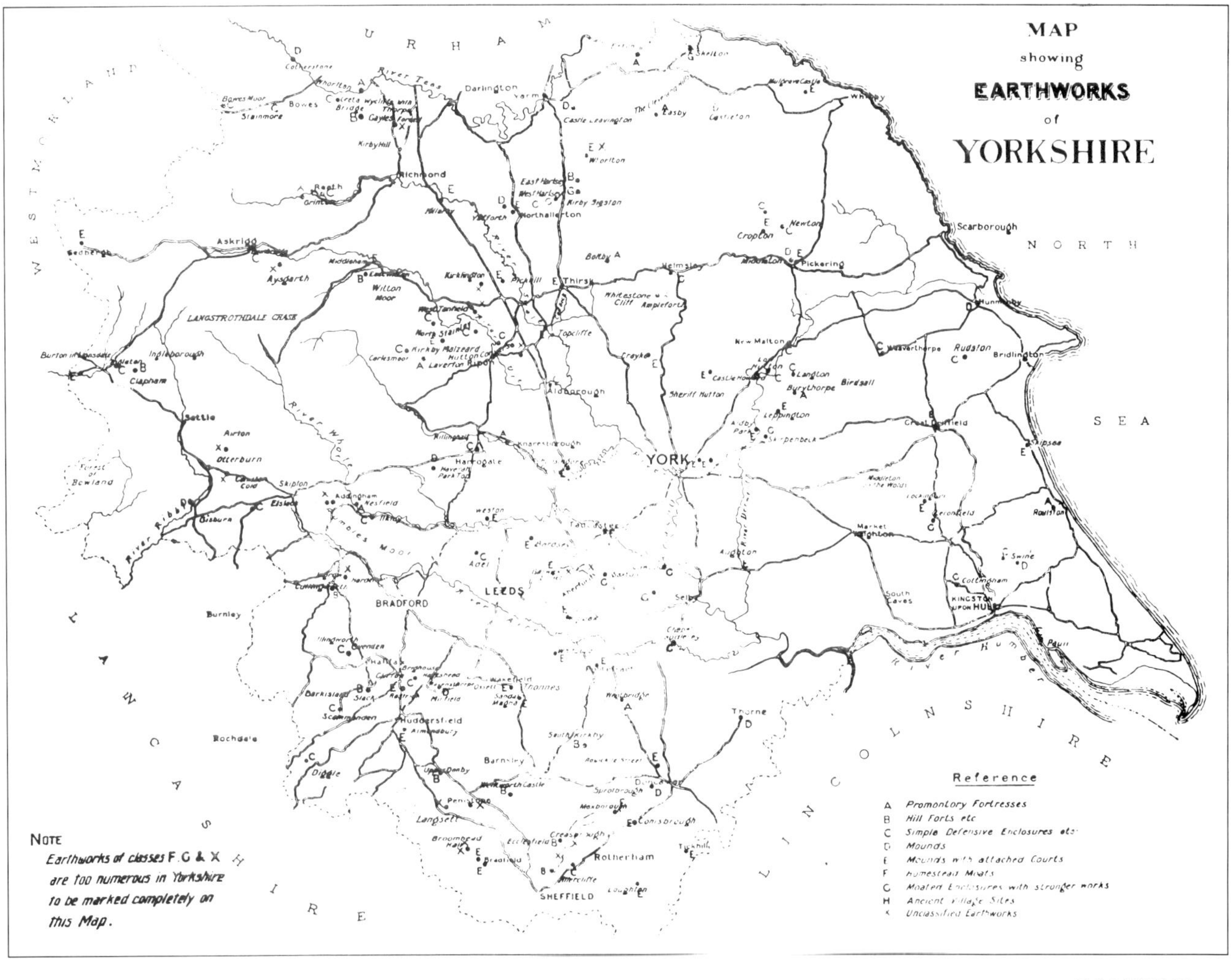

Map showing the earthworks of Yorkshire. *Victoria County History of the County of Yorkshire* (1912).

Ella Armitage c1870, possibly before marriage (Robinson & Thompson, Liverpool).

Ella Armitage, Hon MA of Manchester University, 7 November 1919.

> cate to you as soon as this *Victoria County History* work is off my hands.[1]

She wrote again on 7 July 1907,

> I do not expect to be able to do much more work at castles, as I am getting too old. I have once spoken to Mr Montgomerie of the desirability of forming a small syndicate, of persons like yourself and himself, who are thoroughly interested in castles, and *who are aware how new the subject really is*, for the purpose of publishing a book on castle-building in England to supersede Clark.

Because she was getting on in years – she was then 67 years old – and because interest in castles generally was of a rather vague nature, Ella Armitage, Sands and Montgomerie were never able to organise any kind of castle conference or meeting. But she did get her book on early Norman castles published in 1912 by John Murray and was able to pull together in one volume the enormous amount of work she had done in verifying and listing the castles of the British Isles.

This book, as stated in her letter above, was intended to 'supersede Clark'. But many people nowadays might wonder who Clark was and why he needed superseding. They might wonder, too, what all the fuss was about, nearly one hundred years ago, when historians and archaeologists got heated about castles, castle sites and castle phraseology, when now, thanks very much to Mrs Armitage and her followers, castle studies is an established and respectable subject for students to be interested in. It certainly was not always so. Castles, genuine and otherwise had been lumped together in people's minds as 'ancient monuments', 'mounts' or 'mounds'. As we all know, many of the earliest castles were kept in constant occupation, then lost their strictly military purpose, becoming, for example, royal residences – such as the Tower of London and Windsor Castle. Others collapsed into ruins and in time became covered with grass and shrubs with the memory of their existence becoming folklore. Henry VIII's dissolution of the monasteries and Oliver Cromwell's various destructions all added to the interesting piles of ruins and grassy mounds scattered all over the countryside.

EARLY DESCRIPTIONS OF CASTLES

There had been some attempts over the centuries to enumerate English castles. The late David Cathcart King in the first chapter of his *Castellarium Anglicanum* reckons that Gervase of Canterbury, in the early thir-

Pevensey Castle by S & N Buck 1737.

teenth century, set himself the task of listing what was then existing but only reckoned up to one hundred and then counted two of them twice! John Leland, the antiquary, (born in London about 1506) was one of the 'greats' in his eyes. Leland, who had studied many languages both in England and France, became Henry VIII's librarian and in 1533 was made 'King's Antiquary'. He undertook a tour of England from 1536 to 1542 to observe and note everything he could about monuments and persons. He was an avid collector of information, which he compiled in notebooks he called his *Itineries*. According to *The Dictionary of National Biography*, 'his antiquarian studies overtaxed his brain and he became incurably insane.' His *Itinieries* were not published in his lifetime but have become a wonderful source of information to those willing to look for it. Cathcart King found that Leland mentioned at least 490 certain castles in them.

In the eighteenth century, public taste began to turn to the Gothick and Romantic. The brothers Samuel and Nathaniel Buck fostered this by their prints of castles, abbeys and stately homes in 1737 which were very popular and still are to this very day. As drawings, they are of great value to the modern castellologist. In 1739, Edward King produced the first of four mighty books called *Munimenta Antiqua or Observations on Ancient Castles*. These were filled with drawings of antiquities and naturally included a fair sample of castles as they were in his day.

The accompanying text, however, is full of factual mistakes and this was already recognized in his lifetime. The books, though beautiful to look at, were rather a jumble of information including remarks on the whole progress of architecture from earliest days. Volume III is of especial interest in the study of castles because in this he dealt with Saxon and early Norman material.

Besides these two sources of visual information on castles, there had been a number of detailed works by various learned persons among the growing number of 'antiquarian tourists' – to quote Cathcart King – such as Archdeacon Coxe with his *Historical Tour in Monmouthshire* and James Moore in 1786 and 1798 with his *List of Principal Castles and Monasteries in Great Britain* which contained 530 castles and fortified towers.

In the whole, though, antiquarian subjects, including the study of castles were mainly undertaken by gentlemen (and they were nearly *all* gentlemen – apart from Mrs Armitage and one or two others) with time on their hands and money to spare, as well as having the inclination to dig and explore. Archaeology in all its branches in Britain during the late eighteenth and most of the nineteenth centuries was not at all well organised. Things were different on the Continent. Mrs Armitage was to complain frequently about the state of affairs in the press and in her private correspondence. She considered that 'archaeology was still in its infancy in England, and that it must be confessed that the infancy was a long one.'[2]

MRS ARMITAGE AND THE GROWTH OF ARCHAEOLOGY

But before going any further perhaps it would be as well to explain how Mrs Armitage and a group of her contemporaries and like-minded colleagues fit into the scene just over one hundred years ago. She was born in Liverpool in 1841, the second daughter in a family of fourteen children. Her father, Samual Marshall Bulley was a cotton-broker and her mother was first cousin-once-removed of Sir Stamford Raffles of Singapore. Her paternal aunt, Mary, married a Joshua Wilson of Tunbridge Wells, a rich barrister, who in turn, was related to William Bateman and his son Thomas of Middleton Hall, Youlgrave, Derby. These two were antiquarian barrow-diggers and their many finds are now housed in Sheffield Museum. Joshua Wilson, along with Ella's grandfather, Rev Thomas Raffles, were also keen antiquarians and collectors of curiosities. Both men were to give Ella the run of their large libraries, so she grew up in an atmosphere conducive to learning and finding out about things even though she had no formal education as we now know it. It so happened, however, that she and her immediate sisters (and there were six of them altogether at the head of the family) had an exceptionally good governess. But when she retired, Ella had to take over the task of teaching her eight younger brothers and sisters before they were sent to boarding school in their teens.

This task greatly irked her but she found time, nevertheless, to teach herself many languages and to explore many branches of history. She settled for archaeology with Anglo-Saxon *burhs* and early Norman castles as her chief interests. In 1871 she was accepted as one of the first five students at Newnham College, Cambridge and was, in fact, their first research student, allowed to read in the university library, a privilege much envied by her fellow students. She married the Rev Elkanah Armitage at the comparatively late age of thirty-three but plunged straight away into being a good clergyman's wife, a good mother and a good historian. Her first history book, *The Childhood of the English Nation*, published by Longmans, Green & Co appeared in 1877 very soon after the birth of her two children. Though she helped her husband a great deal in his parish work and later did much in the field of education by sitting on local School Boards and acting, in 1894, as Assistant Commissioner to the Royal Commission on Secondary Education, her research into and reading on history continued unabated. Her reading list for those years is amazing and over the years she collated all the material she obtained from it into a series of notebooks which are now housed in the Yorkshire Archaeological Society's archives in Leeds. When Stubbs' editions of the *Rolls Series* appeared from 1864 in fifteen volumes and his *Select Charters*, the most widely used of all his publications, in 1870, she must have pounced on each volume eagerly. Her granddaughter remembers the parcels of books arriving from The London Library and Ella refers frequently to that Library in her correspondence.

As a result of her study of languages and her wide reading she was able to discover how badly the practice of archaeology in the British Isles compared with that on the Continent – particularly in the Scandinavian countries. She came to admire Dr Sophus Müller, a Danish archaeologist, the author of a work called *Vor Oldtid* which she often quoted. As she wrote in a letter to Goddard Orpen, the Irish historian and fellow castellologist in 1911,

> I am afraid the 'great historical insight' with which you credit me is really due to Dr Sophus Müller, the great Danish archaeologist, as I have acknowledged whenever I have quoted him. In his great work *Vor Oldtid* he has a chapter on the Danish earthworks, including mottes, which I have found most illuminating.[3]

And in the Introduction to her book on castles she quotes him again, as he wrote in his book: 'the fortresses of prehistoric times are the defences of the *community* north of the Alps as in the old classical lands. Small castles for an individual and his warrior-band belong to the Middle Ages.'

Another Danish writer she admired and often quoted was Herr Steenstrup, the author of *Normannerne*, though she admits he was not an archaeologist. But it is evident that Scandinavian writers – archaeologists or not – were well ahead in detailed and systematic work on earthworks. Another of them, J J A Worsaae (1821–85) travelled about Europe extensively and in 1858 published a book – *Recollections* – describing his findings. In it he makes the wise remark,

> Scandinavian countries had so well organised their museums compared with the German, English, French and Southern European countries because the latter had their interests in archaeology absorbed by their numerous Roman monuments, while national monuments were neglected. He saw a connection between the early development of archaeology in Northern Europe and the fact that this region had not been included in Rome's sphere of influence.'[4]

G T CLARK

Then 1884 saw the publication of G T Clark's *Medieval Military Architecture*. Cathcart King likened Clark to John Leyland as being one of the 'giants' – which he undoubtedly was in many respects. His two-volume book was impressive, filled with an enormous amount of information and very

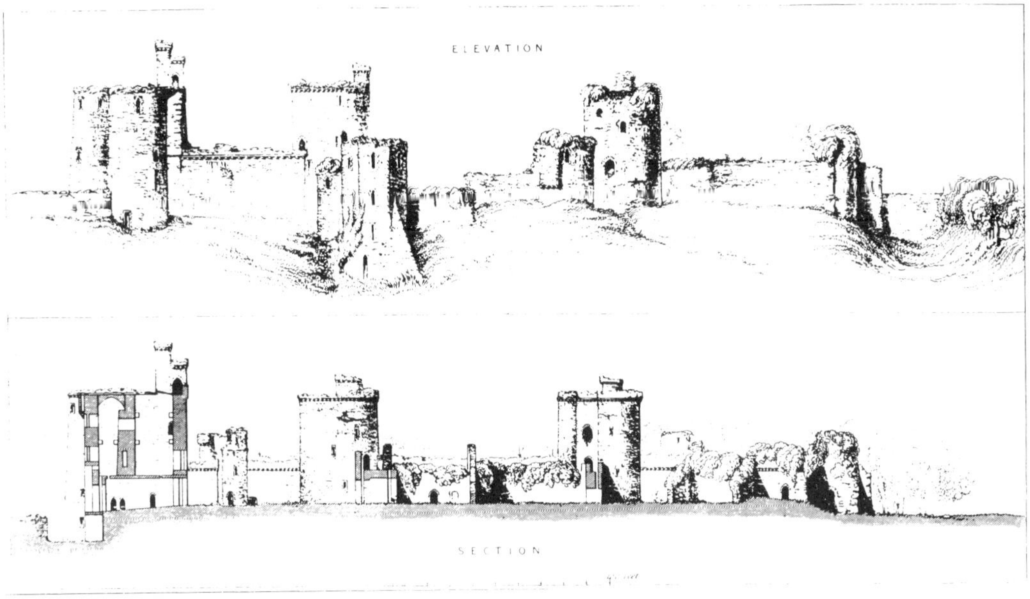

A typical fine engraving from Clark, *Medieval Military Architecture.*

fine drawings and plans of castles in England. But some of the conclusions he came to, especially on the origin of mottes, were later proved to be quite wrong. After a few years, when the impact of his book was beginning to be felt, several people, including Mrs Armitage went into the attack.

Now at that time the historian E A Freeman and John Horace Round, who was an archivist and expert on charters, were embattled in the learned press over their differing views on the Normans and the Norman Conquest. Freeman, another of those magnificently energetic Victorian writers, had brought out his *History of the Norman Conquest* (1867–77) in five volumes. He viewed the Conquest in a peculiarly Victorian way and was ardently pro-Anglo-Saxon and anti-Norman. Round objected strongly to his version of events leading to the Battle of Hastings and did not hesitate to let him know this in articles and letters to the various leading journals interested in such matters. Mrs Armitage in her youth had admired and been influenced by Freeman, both in his ideas and in his prose. But as the years went by she gradually formed her own opinions on the Anglo-Saxon *versus* Norman scene and when she found that Freeman not only approved Clark's motte theories but supported them in print, she was disturbed. She joined with Round in trying to put Clark right.

Clark was not a professional historian but had a great interest in antiquities and curiosities. He originally worked under I K Brunel on the Great Western Railway, then on the Indian railways before returning to England about 1848 as a sub-commissioner following the first Sanitary Act at that time. But in his travels about England and in his spare time he collected a mass of information about anything that caught his fancy. Though as a fine draughtsman with a good eye for detail, he produced illustrations which are most useful, he had not the historical knowledge to fit his findings into their correct slots.

Round had a distinctive view of 'antiquities' and history. He did not have to earn his own living as a young man and was, at first, a bit of a dabbler. But he soon found himself drawn towards investigating family pedigrees and the newly-edited charters. As F M Stenton was to write of him in the *Dictionary of National Biography* after his death in 1928, 'he was the first modern historian to base a narrative on charters and all subsequent use of these materials has been influenced directly or indirectly by his work.'[5]

Though Clark's book had come out in 1884, a review by Round did not appear in print until 1894 when he wrote at length about it in *the Quarterly Review*. He remarked on 'the chaotic beliefs that had prevailed on the subject of castles' and how much 'Castle Clark had done for a branch of study which had remained in a singularly backward state'. He goes on, however, to warn his readers that 'in using his volumes it is as well to remember that their historical side is the weaker, and distinctly inferior, to the architectural.'[6] But the deficiencies in Clark's history set Round, Ella Armitage and several others (to be discussed in more detail at a later date) on a determination to put matters right. Round wrote a long paper in *Archaeologia* in 1902 entitled 'The Castles of the Conquest' and Ella went off on a tour that same year to see for herself how Clark's descriptions and conclusions tallied with the

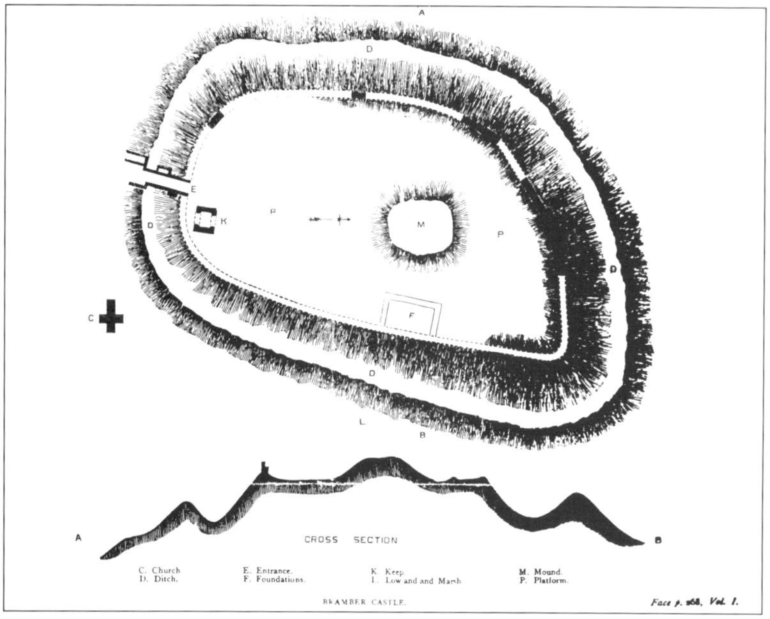

Bramber Castle, plan from G T Clark, *Medieval Military Architecture*.

facts as known through the Pipe Rolls and Charters she had studied. She visited Lewes, Bramber, Arundel, Pevensey and Hastings in Sussex all within a short time in 1902.

SUSSEX CASTLES

Lewes disappointed her a bit when she found the castle bailey was all cut up into houses and gardens. She noted, of course, that the castle was one of the very few in England with two distinct mottes. She noted that the northern motte had a court 26 × 30 paces, and part of an ancient wall (of flint) round this ward, with two mural towers. 'Clark actually wrote of these as Norman!' she exclaimed in her notes. She decided they were very likely to be of the reign of Edward III.

Bramber was visited on 13 November and she realised at once that what Clark called a keep (marked as such on his plan opposite p268, Vol I) is undoubtedly a gatehouse. She remarked that the Church of St Nicholas close by, confirms an early Norman diagnosis of a gatehouse. That it was certainly early Norman and that it had originally been cruciform. She had visited Arundel on 10 November and wrote the long careful description in her notes and later in her book which we have come to expect of her. She expressed her doubts about Clark's use of the term 'shell-keep' for the keep on top of the motte in the centre of the castle complex. But Allen Brown has since discovered that she got the dating wrong for this keep. He announced this almost shame-facedly at the 1982 Anglo-Norman Battle Conference as if he had caught her in some wicked deed!

Her ideas about Pevensey in 1902 had to be amended considerably later because in 1908 her correspondence with Harold Sands referred to the unexpected find he made there while on a dig. It was indeed quite a find and it would be useful at this point to show how archaeological excavations were organised over eighty years ago. A Committee of interested persons got together to raise enough money to excavate the ruins of Pevensey Castle to start in March 1906. Mr Salzman was to be responsible for the Roman side of the excavations, while Mr Sands assisted by Mr Montgomerie concentrated on all things Norman. The Sussex Archeological Society at that time was a bit hard up as they were in the process of buying the Barbican at Lewes Castle (now their headquarters) so were only able to subscribe £5. In all £70 was collected and spent on the digging in 1906 up to 1908 when the Report to the Committee members was published. In this Report, written by Sands, he mentions the fact that Mr G T Clark had paid a short visit to the castle in 1882 and compiled a very inaccurate account of it which appeared in *The Builder* of that year. There had, apparently, been a great mound along the eastern side of the castle in a plan drawn by a Mr Figg in 1802 which had also appeared as 'a lofty mound' in King's *Munimenta Antiqua* of 1801. Sands reported that the legend of this mound had been fostered ever since by writers of the school of Freeman and Clark. Sands, unfortunately, does not say what they thought this mound was but even Mrs Armitage had mistaken it for a motte. Much to her and everyone's delight and surprise, Sands found it to be a Norman keep whose ruins, over the years, had been completely buried by rubbish and earth. She wrote to Sands on 12 March 1908, 'I am so much obliged to you in telling me

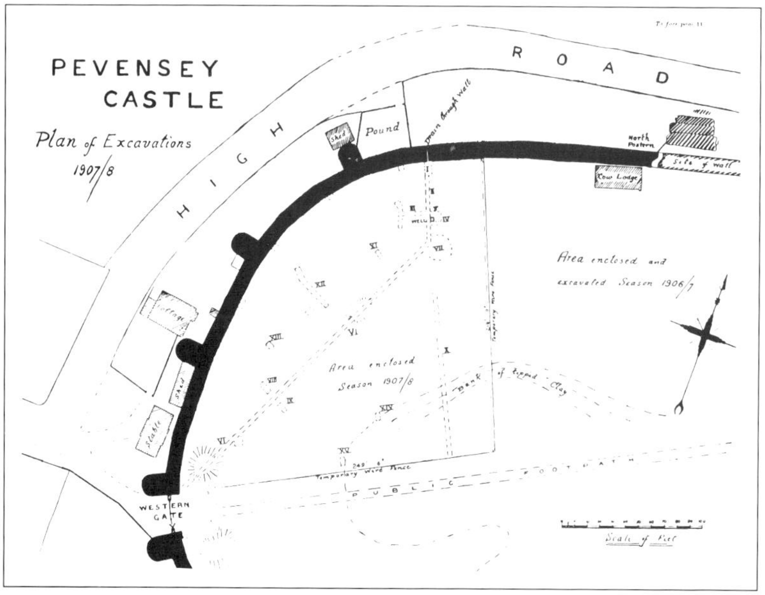

Pevensey Castle, plan of the excavations by Harold Sands from the report to the Excavation Committee, 1908.

about this wonderful discovery at Pevensey so fully. Mr Montgomerie is indeed lucky to be in on this . . . Who can say how many other early Norman keeps may not be buried beneath the soil?'[1]

She went on to Hastings on the 14th – a castle to be the object of another of Sands' digs later on. But in 1902 nothing new had been discovered though she again found herself disagreeing with Clark's ideas. She had already noted a gateway of Edward I's time but 'the present main gateway' as she wrote in her notes 'Clark had said was protected by a late tower with slight walls and a flanking wall projecting about 20 feet'. A gatekeeper told her that this gate had been built up from fragments, and she certainly thought it hardly likely that there were two gateways to so small a castle and held that the Edwardian one was on the original site.

PREPARATION AND PUBLICATION

By now she had begun to compile her own list of early Norman castles. But just before then, in March 1900, her cousin, Professor Gerard Baldwin Brown, had read a paper for her to the Society of Antiquaries of Scotland. He held the Chair of Fine Arts at Edinburgh University. This paper clearly stated what both she and Round had found wrong with Clark's opinions on the origins of many castles in England. She wrote:

> . . . finding that in several places where the Anglo-Saxon records tell of *burhs* or strongholds erected by our forefathers, there are still existing round hillocks of earth, surrounded with ditches, he jumped to the conclusion that a *burh* was a moated hillock, and then proceeded to assert that it was so, without any further inquiry into the literary history of the word . . . strange to say this very scanty and disputable evidence has been accepted without question even by such writers as Freeman and Green, and is adopted by most of the antiquarian books and papers written during the last twenty years.[7]

She goes on in her paper to show the differences between the Anglo-Saxon *burhs* (or fortified enclosures) and early Norman mottes, carefully listing the *burhs* of Ethelfleda and Edward the Elder and showing where a subsequent Norman castle had been built in or near them. This is now common knowledge to the modern student of castles, but ninety years ago, when as I have already said, there was no coherent work done on castles and castle sites, it was all rather exciting.

In 1904 she wrote two long articles for *The English Historical Review* as a result of her travels about England. This listed fifty castles

Pevensey Castle excavations by Harold Sands – North Postern. (By courtesy of hastings Museum)

mentioned in the Domesday Book. She wanted to check Clark's favourite theory that moated mounds were the centres of large and important estates in pre-conquest Saxon times. She drew up a table of all the different sites showing whether they had gone up in value since before the conquest and discovered that his theory was but a dream. 'Out of forty-one mottes in country districts thirty-six are found in places which were quite insignificant in King Edward's day, and only five can be said to occupy the centre of important Saxon manors.'[8] This article, with the paper given for her in Scotland, plus a lengthy article in the *Antiquary* of 1906 on 'The Norman Origin of Irish Mottes' (of which more anon in a later article) form the basis of the book which is still considered a major work – *The Early Norman Castles of the British Isles* published by John Murray in 1912.

While she was preparing her book for the

Pevensey Castle excavations by Harold Sands – timber structure (?well lining). (By courtesy of Hastings Museum)

printers, another useful book on earthworks was published by Macmillan & Co in 1908 for A Hadrian Allcroft, MA. Its title was *Earthworks of England* and in it he described in words and diagrams the many kinds of earthworks – Prehistoric, Roman, Saxon, Danish, Norman and Medieval – scattered all over England. This work had been inspired, no doubt, by the work being done and classified by the Committee on Ancient Earthworks and Fortified Enclosures because, in his Preface he outlined their aims. The Committee 'has been working to educate the nation in the value and significance of its earthworks, to obtain complete lists and authoritative plans of all, and preserve them where possible from the destruction which daily threatens them.'[9] He had good words, too, to say about the publishers of *The Victoria County Histories* for their inclusion of a study of the earthworks of each county and thought they deserved the gratitude of all archeologists.

Between the time Mrs Armitage's paper on castles was read for her in Edinburgh in 1900 and the time her final book came out in 1912 there had certainly been an improvement in the organisation of archaeological subjects – including castle sites. I Chalkey Gould was the Hon Secretary to the Committee on Ancient Earthworks and Fortified Enclosures when the Congress of Archaeological Societies met in July 1907 (both Round and Montgomerie were on the committee). In February of that year Gould wrote to E Kitson Clark, the Hon Librarian of the Yorkshire Archaeological Society telling him that his friend Montgomerie was working with Mrs Armitage of Rawden and had already completed a very long list of Yorkshire earthworks for *The Victoria County History.* He wondered if the people of the VCH would allow the Yorkshire Archeological Society to use the list.[10]

Compiling this list of all the earthworks arranged in the nine different classes drawn up by the Earthworks Committee of the Congress of Archaeological Societies must have been an arduous task. Castles, as they are now simply called, fell into classes D and E – as forts and fortified mounts. There was then still great uncertainty about these origins among the general public so Mrs Armitage had to preface her findings with the remark, 'the evidence for their Norman origin appears to us too strong to be gainsaid but of course cannot be discussed here.' Yorkshire then was treated as one whole county and the accompanying map will give an idea of the vast amount of work entailed in cataloguing the many earthworks in such a large area. Each earthwork, mount or castle was carefully described by her and she gave documentary evidence in the case of standing castles to prove their Norman origins. Montgomerie provided plans to illustrate many of the sites she described.

In January 1908, in the report of the Earthworks Committee to the Council, thanks were given to Montgomerie for his help in preparing the schedule for *The Victoria County History* article. It was sad there was no record of thanks to Mrs Armitage for her contribution to this article, but in 1919 Manchester University awarded her an Honorary MA for her services to archaeology.

ENGLISH CASTLES STUDIES SINCE ELLA ARMITAGE

The publication of *The Victoria County Histories* did a great deal to arouse general public interest in the importance of preserving and maintaining castles and other historic buildings. Sir Charles Reed Peers (1868–1952) was another man who had much to do with this pioneering work. In 1903 he had been appointed architectural editor in the newly formed team bringing out these volumes. After his death, Mortimer Wheeler wrote of him in *The Dictionary of National Biography*, 'the high reputation acquired by these Histories as an architectural record was in considerable measure his creation.'[12] In 1910, Sir Charles was appointed Inspector of Monuments in the Office of Works. His first task was to advise on the reform of the Ancient Monuments Act of 1882 and a new Act in 1913 enlarged the powers of the Commissioners of Works to conserve ancient structures. He became Chief Inspector of Ancient Monuments, the first in a line of distinguished Chief Inspectors. He retired in 1933.

The First World War interrupted much of the archaeological and other serious castle study work which had started at the beginning of this century and the Second War coming so soon after the First also slowed down considerably any advance which might have been made in conjunction with the Office of Works – later the Department of the Environment. However, since the 1950s, there has been a great upsurge of interest in castles and the archaeology connected with them. HMSO (Her Majesty's Stationery Office), for example, brought out many booklets on individual castles and in 1963 Vols I and II of *The History of the Kings' Works* appeared. This was written jointly by H M Colvin, A J Taylor and R Allen Brown. A number of serious studies and articles appeared regularly – too many to enumerate here. The major international get-together of castle specialists or castellologists as they are now called was founded in 1962. This was the *Chateau Gaillard* bi-annual conference already described by Christine Mahany in the first number of *Fortress*. Then in 1978 the late Professor Allen Brown, now so sadly missed, inaugurated the annual Anglo-Norman Studies conference at Battle, East Sussex, on the site of the Norman victory at Hastings, where all aspects of the Norman way of life are discussed. Castles and visits to castles naturally play a large part in the proceedings.

A new group – *The Castles Studies Group* – with Dr R A Higham of Exeter University as acting secretary held its first meeting in April 1987. The aim of this British-based group is to promote and communicate current research on castles. A Newsletter is produced every autumn and it is surprising how fast membership is growing – or, perhaps, it is not surprising as once bitten by the castle-study bug it is difficult not to stay with it for a long time. I must end by quoting once more from Mrs Armitage. She ends a long letter to Sands in July 1907 in which she discussed the escape of Ranulf Flambard from the Tower of London in 1101 with these words 'But I *must* stop – it is so difficult to stop when one is writing about castles!'

Footnotes

1. All letters from Mrs Armitage to Harold Sands quoted here are in the possession of the Society of Antiquaries, London.,
2. Mrs E S Armitage, *Yorkshire Archaeological Journal* xiii (1895), pp35–43.
3. Mrs E S Armitage, letter to Goddard Orpen, 14 September 1911, in the possession of the National Library of Ireland, ms 17784.
4. Bo Gräsland, *The Birth of Prehistoric Chronology* (Cambridge, 1987), p15 (Gräsland's précis of Worsaae's words).
5. F Stenton, *Dictionary of National Biography*, vol 1922–1930, p731.
6. J H Round, *Quarterly Review* 179 (July and October 1894), pp27–29.
7. Mrs E S Armitage, *Proceedings of the Society of Antiquaries of Scotland* (March 1900), pp260–61.
8. Mrs E S Armitage, *English Historical Review* xix (1904), pp450–55.
9. A Hadrian Allcroft, ma, *Earthwork of England*, *Macmillan & Co Ltd*, (London 1908), Preface, viii.
10. I Chalkey Gould, letter to Kitson Clark dated February 1907, in the possession of the Yorkshire Archaeological Society.
11. Mrs E S Armitage, *Victoria County History of the County of York*, part II (London 1912), p19.
12. Mortimer Wheeler, *Dictionary of National Biography*, vol 1951–1960, p800.

Arundel Castle. Visit of the Anglo-Norman Studies Conference (Battle), 1982. (*author*)

There are numerous good books on fortifications which, for one reason or another, do not receive widespread distribution in this country. It is our intention to offer selected titles as a service to our readers. This list will be continuously expanded as new publications come to our attention, and we welcome suggestions from readers, providing they can supply title, author and publisher (as well as ISBN number if possible). However, no book can be ordered until it appears on this list. The current selection is as follows:

BS3/1
L'Architecture Militaire Grecque
by Jean-Pierre Adam
See earlier issues for details.
300 x 225mm, 264 pages, 428 illustrations.
£58.00

BS1/1
Bulwark of Empire: Bermuda's Fortified Naval Base
by Roger Willock
See the review in *Fortress* 1 for details.
192 pages, 17 illustrations. **£15.00**

BS3/2
Burgenkunde
by Otto Piper
See earlier issues for details.
270 x 180mm, 732 pages, 633 illustrations.
£48.00

BS2/1
Byzantine Fortifications: An Introduction
by Clive Foss & David Winfield
See the review in *Fortress* 3 for details.
316 pages, 233 illustrations. **£25.00**

BS4/1
Castellarium Anglicanum
by D J Cathcart King
The late David King's masterwork, a catalogue and related bibliography of every castle site in England and Wales – extant, vanished, possibles, rejects and related structures, whether earthwork or stone. Every serious castellologist must have a copy of this book, despite its high price.
255 x 175mm, 2 vols totalling 736 pages, 23 photographs, 60 maps.
£125.00 for a 2-volume set (allow 8–10 weeks for delivery)

BS3/3
Castelli, Rocche e Mura d'Italia
by Gian Maria Tabarelli
See earlier issues for details.
305 x 240mm, 260 pages, 545 illustrations.
£48.00

BS5/1
Castles and Cannon
by B H St J O'Neil
Bryan O'Neil's pioneering study of early artillery fortifications in England, available once again in this limited edition.
230 x 150mm, 144 pages, 80 illustrations.
£35.00

BS2/2
Discovering the Fortifications of the Order of St John in Malta
by Stephen C Spiteri
This book is now out of print; no more orders please until further notice.

BS2/3
Encyclopedia of Historic Forts
by Robert B Roberts
See review in *Fortress* 2 for details.
894 pages, 181 illustrations. **£94.00*** (allow 8–10 weeks for delivery)

BS1/3
Festungsbaukunst und Festungsbautechnik
by Hartwig Neumann
See *Fortress* 1 for details.
440 pages. **£55.00**

BS6/1
Firearms & Fortifications: Military Architecture and Siege Warfare in Sixteenth Century Siena
by Simon Pepper and Nicholas Adams
Traces the evolving relationship between attack and defence, siege warfare and military architecture, using the experiences of Siena in the period 1525–55 as a case study.
253 × 175mm, 272 pages, 87 illustrations.
£23.00

BS2/4
Las Fortificaciones del Periodo Hispánico en Venezuela
by Graziano Gasparini
See *Fortress* 2 for details.
260 x 230mm, 336 pages, *c*250 illustrations.
£42.00* (including airmail postage)

BS1/2
The Fortifications of Armenian Cilicia
by Robert W Edwards
See review in *Fortress* 1 for further details.
622 pages, 428 illustrations **£45.00***

BS6/2
Fortress America: The Corps of Engineers, Hampton Roads, and United States Coastal Defense
by David A Clary
A survey of US coast defence policy, procurement and equipment since independence, concentrating on the role of the Engineers.
235 × 158mm, 224 pages, 25 illustrations.
£34.00

Guides des Châteaux de France
(series – various authors)
See the review in *Fortress* 2 for further details; the full list is as follows:

BS2/5	**Aveyron**, 80 pages, 75 châteaux described	£5.00
BS2/6	**Cote d'Or**, 182 pages, 140 châteaux described	£6.00
BS2/7	**Dordogne**, 142 pages, 180 châteaux described	£6.00
BS2/8	**Gers**, 160 pages, 146 châteaux described	£6.00
BS2/9	**Gironde**, 174 pages, 231 châteaux described	£6.00
BS2/10	**Landes**, 80 pages, 43 châteaux described	£5.00
BS2/11	**Lot**, 80 pages, 70 châteaux described	£5.00
BS2/12	**Lot-et-Garonne**, 80 pages, 76 châteaux described	£5.00
BS2/13	**Meurthe-et-Moselle**, 144 pages, 220 châteaux described	£6.00
BS2/14	**Moselle**, 160 pages, 189 châteaux described	£6.00
BS2/15	**Niévre**, 104 pages, 103 châteaux described	£5.00
BS2/16	**Nord**, 184 pages, 160 châteaux described	£6.00
BS2/17	**Pas-de-Calais**, 220 pages, 226 châteaux described	£6.00
BS2/18	**Pyrenees-Atlantiques**, 80 pages, 68 châteaux described	£5.00
BS2/19	**Bas-Rhin**, 184 pages, 225 châteaux described	£6.00
BS2/20	**Haut-Rhin**, 176 pages, 202 châteaux described	£6.00
BS2/21	**Saone-et-Loire**, 190 pages, 198 châteaux described	£6.00
BS2/22	**Yonne**, 144 pages, 109 châteaux described	£6.00
BS2/23	**Region Provence – Cote d'Azur**, 136 pages, 235 châteaux described	£9.00
BS2/24	**Region Centre – Val de Loire**, 168 pages, 318 châteaux described	£9.00

BS5/2
Die Klassizistische Grossfestung Koblenz
by Hartwig Neumann & Udo Liessem
A detailed and heavily illustrated study of the elaborate nineteenth century fortifications of this stategic Rheinland town. To be reviewed in *Fortress* 7.
260 x 200mm, 144 pages. **£22.00**

BS5/3
Seul Entre Meuse et Ourthe: Le Fort de Boncelles
by Michel Viatour
A technical and historical account of the Belgian Brialmont fort at Boncelles, essentially between August 1914 and May 1940, but including its construction and fitting-out. In French.
296 x 205mm, 170 pages plus 112 pages of illustrations, specifications and appendix matter. **£20.00**

*Note price increases (from May 1990).

The prices quoted include post and packing. Please note that books are not stocked, but will be dispatched direct from the publisher by ordinary surface mail unless stated otherwise so delivery times may be protracted. Please give BS number references with order; payment must be made in advance by postal order, personal cheque or Visa/Mastercard (Access) credit cards (quote number, expiry date and home address). Cheques and money orders should be made out to Beaufort Publishing Ltd. This service is available only to paid-up subscribers to *Fortress*.

REVIEWS

R Allen Brown, *Castles, Conquest and Charters. Collected Papers*, published by The Boydell Press (Woodbridge 1989).
180 × 250mm, 387 pages, 74 illustrations.
ISBN 0 85115 524 3.
£49.50.

The title given to this collection of twenty-six papers by the late Professor Allen Brown sums up their range. They speak for themselves without introduction and are straight reprints from a wide array of publications which include French and Italian as well as the more familiar British historical and archaeological learned journals.

The collection begins with 'An Historian's Approach to the Origins of the Castle in England' from *The Archaeological Journal* of 1970, which was stimulated by the Royal Archaeological Institute's research project into the origins of castles, and the suggestion that had been made in the course of it that we might look for the antecedents of the castle in the private fortified residences of late-Saxon England. The article includes Brian Davison's response to this polemic, emphasizing the nature of the contribution archaeology could perhaps bring to the problem. Linked to this is the paper which introduced the 1966 Château Gaillard conference at Battle, 'The Norman Conquest and the Genesis of English Castles'.

The next article is 'Royal Castle-Building in England, 1154–1216', *English Historical Review* (1955) which reflected Allen Brown's postgraduate research and pointed to his contribution to *The History of the King's Works* (1963). It is followed by 'A List of Castles, 1154–1616' also in *EHR* (1959). There then comes a number of wide-ranging articles on castle themes: 'The Castles of the Conquest', *Domesday Book Studies*, eds A Williams and R W H Erskine (London 1987); 'Châteaux et sociétiés du xive au xvie siècle', *Châteaux et sociétiés du xive au xvie: Notes des premières recontres internationales d'arche, d'histoire de Commarques*, ed P Fanlac (Perigueuex 1986); 'Les châteaux féodaux', *Cahiers de civilisation médiévale xxix (1986); 'Lo Studio dei Castelli Medievali in Inghilterra', Castelli: storia e archeologia*, eds Rinaldo Combia & Aldo A-Settia (Turin 1984); 'Le manoir fortifié dans le royaume d'Angleterre', *La maison forte au moyen âge*, ed M Bur (Paris 1986); 'Some Observations on the Tower of London', *Archaeological Journal* (1979); 'The White Tower of London', *The Cambridge Guide to the Arts in Britain* (Cambridge 1988); 'Framlingham Castle and Bigod 1154–1216', *Proceedings of the Suffolk Institute of Archaeology* (1951); 'A Note on Kenilworth Castle: The Change to Royal Ownership', *Archaeological Journal* (1954); 'The Architecture of the Bayeux Tapestry', *The Bayeux Tapestry*, ed F M Stenton (London 1959).

Criccieth – one of the illustrations from Paul Johnson's new book, reviewed overleaf.

Wider architectural and historical subjects, including his work on early charters, cover: 'William of Malmesbury as an Architectural Historian', 'Castle Gates and Garden Gates', 'King Edward's Clocks', 'The Norman Conquest', 'The Battle of Hastings', 'The Status of the Norman Knight', 'Guillaume le Conquérant et son temps', 'The Public Records and the Historian', 'The "Treasury" of the Later Twelfth Century', 'Early Charters of Sibton Abbey, Suffolk', and 'Some Observations on Norman and Anglo-Saxon Charters'. Finally and most appropriately, there is 'Too Many Mansions', Allen Brown's Inaugral Lecture at King's College, University of London. There he fittingly set out his philosophy and fears for the teaching of history in his characteristic forthright style.

This book provides a most valuable service for those not in reach of a major library. Indeed, it is unlikely that any library will contain all this material. The price is high and the quality of the reproduction, as might be expected in the circumstances, is not always consistent, notably with some of the illustrations. This is, however, a book which many will need in order to put beside those stimulating, authoritative and enjoyable books by that master of castle studies, R Allen Brown.

Andrew Saunders

T J Hoekstra, M D de Weerd and S L Wynia (eds), *Het Romeinse Castellum te Utrecht*, numerous contributors
265 × 185mm, 192 pages, 110 illustrations.
ISBN 90 71366 16 2.
Paperback

This volume is the first full publication of excavations in the Roman levels of the fort at Utrecht undertaken between 1936 and 1949 by A E van Giffen. Utrecht, the *Traiectum* of the Antonine Itinerary, was one of the permanent installations on the lower Rhine *limes*, and although the publication of work at other sites in the same area such as Nijmegen, Vechten, Valkenburg and Zwammerdam have made them better known, this account seeks to set the record straight. Even so, the report does not deal with any of the complex post-Roman remains found on the site, claimed to have been in continuous occupation since AD 47.

Early chapters deal with the methods the writers have used in their work on the excavation records, and with the history of research into Utrecht's Roman past. These are followed by an attempt to set Utrecht into the emerging historical framework of research into the lower Rhine *limes* as a whole. Then the book settles down to give first a concise, then a more extended account of the series of Roman forts which occupied the site, followed by a selection of finds which include decorated and stamped Samian wares, a copious supply of tile-stamps, graffiti, and a small amount of metalwork. The main text is in Dutch: there are full summaries in English and German; in addition all the 110 illustrations have captions in Dutch and English. A feature of the book is the publication, virtually unaltered, of the excavator's original record plans of the site.

The main part of the book is formed by the chapters in which the six main periods of occupation identified by the excavator are described in detail. Although the account shows the restricted nature of the excavations, the evidence is clearly presented: an earth and timber fort of around 1.17 ha was established by about AD 50 (Period 1). This was rebuilt on the same site three times – once (Period 2) prior to the Batavian revolt in AD 69, the second time (Period 3) shortly after that revolt, and finally (Period 4) in the first quarter of the second century. In about AD 210, a new and larger stone-built fort (Period 5) covering 1.87 ha was erected; its walls, built of tufa, occupied the site of the ditches of the earlier sequence of forts. Its headquarters occupied the position of that of the earlier forts, and was also of stone, though the barracks were of wood. Late Roman finds from the site suggest that there was occupation at a later date (Period 6), though its character is unknown.

The authors themselves candidly ask whether it is worth expending time and effort to publish long outstanding excavations such as these. The answer in this case must be 'yes'! Good archaeological information can never become out of date; moreover, it is always important to demonstrate the extent and the reliability of the evidence on which interpretation is based. This book succeeds in bringing Van Giffen's work to life and in providing another solid platform of archaeological evidence for the Roman frontier on the lower Rhine.

Stephen Johnson

Cooling Castle gateway – an illustration from Paul Johnson's book reviewed here.

PAUL JOHNSON, *Castles of England and Wales*, published by Weidenfeld and Nicholson (London 1989).
260 × 198mm, 215 pages, 126 photographs (71 in colour), 16 plans and maps.
ISBN 0 297 79574 0.
£12.95.

This book is difficult to place. It is not a coffee-table book though the quality of the photography is very high and the choice of illustration often reflects an unfamiliar viewpoint. Nor can it be regarded as a serious contribution to castle studies. If it is simply intended for the general reader as a broad, if lengthy, summary of the development of the castle in mainland Britain, it offers no new insights and is both factually unreliable and out of date in its interpretations. It presents an overview which has been overtaken by Allen Brown, Derek Renn, Stewart Cruden, and others during the past twenty years or so. In design terms, the 'landscape' format makes it a difficult book to read without some form of support.

The contents extend from 'The Norman Yoke' to 'Plantagenet Castles', to 'Edwardian Splendour in Wales' and through to 'The Last of the Feudal Castles', the 'Castles and Towers of the Borders', and thence to 'The Scottish Inheritance'. It subsequently extends its scope to the artillery fortifications of Henry VIII and Elizabeth but lacks any illustration to demonstrate the fundamental change from rounded medieval forms to the Italian-derived angle bastion other than a not entirely accurate plan of Carisbrooke Castle. The Civil War is scantily treated, and then mainly by descriptions of sieges. The final chapter is a brief essay into the survival of castellated forms in eighteenth and nineteenth century domestic architecture.

In historical terms Paul Johnson presents a curious view of monarchy in the Middle Ages which implies a highly centralised system of royal government in which the baronage had little part other than to cause trouble. Castles are seen almost entirely in relation to the king. Of course the king was the principal castle builder and strove to keep the more strategic castles in his control but the extent to which the majority of castles were constructed by the baronage and their feudal tenants is not apparent here.

Old perceptions long ago debunked abound: 'Most of the new ideas in fortification came from the eastern Mediterranean and were brought back to western Europe by crusaders' was an idea demolished by T E Lawrence. Michele Sanmichele is credited with the invention of the angle bastion at Verona! And there are some extraordinary statements for which it is difficult to find a source, such as the claim that Tintagel Castle began as the re-fortifying of a Roman stronghold by the Saxons or that Northumbria 'never had an Iron Age in fortress terms'. The description of Windsor Castle on 'a huge rock' rather than being set on a chalk cliff in the Thames Valley is misleading. Mistakes and oversimpifications are numerous. Many are due to inadequate research in the now extensive literature on the subject. The book is not helped in this respect by the block plans which give the reader little idea of the complicated change and development which affected most castles.

The concept of bringing together the English, Scottish and Welsh castles together when they are so often treated separately is a good one. But the chapter devoted to Scotland is inadequate for such an extensive and complex subject. There is no mention, for example, of the technical advances in artillery fortification during the fifteenth and sixteenth centuries which, for a time, put Scotland ahead of its southern neighbour. The chapter on castles and towers of the Borders is more concerned with anecdotes of raiding. It represents a missed opportunity.

Andrew Saunders

PUBLICATIONS LISTINGS FOR 1990

Books and Monographs

CATHERINE ATKINSON, *Celle – Eine Wehrhafte stadt: Ausgrabung an der ehemaligen Stadtbefestigung vor dem Hintergrund der frühneuzeitlichen Festungsgeschichte*, Bormann-Museum (Celle 1989)
100 pages, 73 illustrations (11 in colour)
No ISBN no. No price.

L R P OZINGA, T J HOEKSTRA, MD DE WEERD, S L WYNIA (eds), *Het Romeinse Castellum Te Utrecht*, Universteit van Amsterdam, Albert Egges van Giffen Instituut Voor Praeen Protohistorie, Studies in Prae-en Protohistorie 3, Broese Kemink (Utrecht 1989).
Reviewed in this issue.

R ALLEN BROWN, *Castles, Conquest & Charters. Collected Papers,* The Boydell Press (Woodbridge 1989).
Reviewed in this issue.

D GABLER (ed) *The Roman Fort at Acs-Vaspuszta (Hungary) on the Danube limes* 2 vols, British Archaeological Reports, (Oxford 1989).
ISBN 0 86054 676 4.
£55.00.

PAUL JOHNSON, *Castles of England, Scotland and Wales* Weidenfeld & Nicholson (London 1989).
Reviewed in this issue.

W H MANNING, *Report on the Excavations at Usk, 1965–1976. The Fortress Excavations, 1972–74*, University of Wales Press (Cardiff 1989).
194 pages, 33 plates, 76 figs.
ISBN 0 7083 1050 8.
£30.00

HARTWIG NEUMANN and UDO LIESSEM, *Die Klassizistische Grossfestung Koblenz*, Bernard & Graefe Verlag (Koblenz 1989).
ISBN 3 7637 5853 4
Available through the Fortress Book Service.

MICHEL VIATOR, *Seul Entre Meuse et Ourthe. Le Fort de Boncelles, Aout 1914 – Mai 1940* (G. Everling, Arlon 2nd ed 1989)
288 pages, 90 plates, 26 figs.
Available through the Fortress Book Service.

G J WIGHTMAN, *The Damascus Gate, Jerusalem* Excavations by C-M Bennett and J B Hennessy at the Damascus Gate, Jerusalem, 1964–66, British Archaeological Reports (Oxford 1989).
ISBN 0 86054 660 8.
£23.00.

Periodical Literature

PETER ARNOLD and R B BURNS, 'The Fort Albert Dig', *Alderney Society Bulletin* 24 (1989), pp23–31.

K BOOTH and J CRONIN, 'Buckton Castle', *The Greater Manchester Archaeological Journal* 3 [1987–88] (1989), pp61–66.

MARK BOWDEN and DAVE MCOMISH, 'Little Boxes: More about hillforts', *Scottish Archaeological Review* 6 (1989), pp12–15.

MARK COLLARD, 'Excavations at Desborough Castle, High Wycombe 1987', *Records of Buckinghamshire* 30 (1988), pp15–41.

BRIAN DEARDEN, 'Charles the Bald's Fortified Bridge at Pitres (Seine). Recent Archaeological Investigations', *Anglo-Norman Studies* 11 (1988), pp107–112.

JAMES L GILLESPIE, 'Dover Castle: Key to Richard II's Kingdom?', *Archaeologia Cantiana* 105 (1988), pp179–196.

CARROLL GILMOR, 'The Logistics of Fortified Bridge Building on the Seine under Charles the Bald', *Anglo-Norman Studies* 11 (1988), pp87–106.

O GIMOUVEZ AND L SCHNEIDER, 'Un castrum des environs de l'An Mil en Languedoc central: le Rocher des Vierges à Saint-Saturnin (Hérault)', *Archéologie du Midi Médiévale* 6 (1988), pp101–122.

GEORGE L GOOD and CHRISTOPHER J TABRAHAM, 'Excavations at Smailholm Tower, Roxburghshire', *Proceedings of the Society of Antiquaries of Scotland* 118 (1988), pp231–266.

PAMELA GREENWOOD, 'Uphall Camp, Ilford, Essex: an Iron Age Fortification', *The London Archaeologist* 6, no 4 (Autumn 1989), pp94–100.

R A HALL, 'The Five Boroughs of the Danelaw: a review of present knowledge', *Anglo Saxon England* 18 (1989), pp 149–208.

VALERIE HORSMAN, 'Eynsford Castle, A reintrpretation of the early history in the light of recent excavations', *Archaeologia Cantiana* 105 (1988), pp39–55.

GAVIN KINSLEY, 'Excavation on the supposed site of Civil War Redoubt 11B, Newark-on-Trent, Nottinghamshire', *Transactions of the Thoroton Society SCII (1988), p78.*

G LEFRANC, F PERREAU, 'Mottes et sites fortifiés médievaux du Pas-de-Calais. Pour la construction d'une documentation topographique', *Bulletin de la Commission Départmentale d'Histoire et d'Archéolgie du Pas-De-Calais* (1989), pp329–344.

C J LYNN, 'Navan Fort: a draft summary of D M Waterman's excavations', *Emania, Bulletin of the Navan Research Group* 1 (1986), pp11–19.

J P MALLORY, 'Trial Excavations at Haughey's Fort' *Emania, Bulletin of the Navan Research Group* 4 (1988), pp5–20.

J P MALLORY and R B WARNER, 'The Date of Haughey's Fort', *Emania, Bulletin of the Navan Research Group* 5 (1988), pp36–39.

J C MANN, 'The history of the Antonine Wall – a reappraisal', *Proceedings of the Society of Antiquaries of Scotland* 118 (1988), pp101–137.

J NOLAN, R FRASER, R B HARBOTTLE and F C BURTON, 'The Medieval Town Defences of Newcastle upon Tyne: Excavation and Survey, 1986–87', *Archaeologia Aeliana* 17 (1989), pp29–78.

A SCHNEIDER, 'Burgen und Befestigungsanlagen des Mittelalters in Bodenseekreis. Eine Bestamdsaufnahme', *Fundserichte am Baden Wurthemberg* 14 (1989), pp515–668.

SELVIU SANIE, 'La citadelle géto-dace de Barbosi', *Archeologia Moldovei* 12 (1988), pp53–104.

STUART D SCOTT and PATRICIA KAY SCOTT, 'In the Field A Fort Called Niagara', *Archaeology* 43 (1), (1990), pp64–67.

GEORGE SMITH, 'Excavation of the Iron Age Cliff Promontory Fort and of Mesolithic and Neolithic flint-working areas at Penhale Point, Holywell Bay, near Newquay, 1983', *Cornish Archaeology* 27 (1988), pp171–199.

D START, N REDHEAD, J ROBERTS, 'Excavation and Conservation at Castleshaw Roman Forts', *The Greater Manchester Archaeological Journal* 3 [1987–88] (1989), pp45–55.

CHRISTOPHER J TABRAHAM, 'The Scottish medieval tower-house as lordly residence in the light of recent excavation', *Proceedings of the Society of Antiquaries of Scotland* 118 (1988), pp267–276.

WADE TARZIA, 'No Trespassing: Border Defence in the Táin Bo Cuailge', *Emania, Bulletin of the Navan Research Group* 3 (1987), pp28–33.

G WEBER, 'Neus zur Befestigung des Oppidums Tarodunum, Gde. Kirchzarten, Kreis Breisgau – Hochschwarzwald', *Fundserichte am Baden Wurthemberg* 14 (1989), pp273–288.

D J WOOLISCROFT, 'Signalling and the design of Hadrian's Wall', *Archaeologia Aeliana* 17 (1989), pp5–20.

Notes on Contributors

Ken Denholm is an Australian and a draughtsman in electrical engineering who has spent thirty years of his life in Africa and has an incurable interest in historical matters. He has spent five years in research on the fortifications of St Helena.

Victor T G Smith is a civil servant currently seconded to be General Manager of the Brimstone Hill Fortress project. He is an authority on the fortifications of the Thames Estuary and the Chatham defences and has extended his academic researches to the fields of practical conservation and restoration, notably at New Tavern Fort, Gravesend, and Coalhouse Fort, East Tilbury. He is Conservation Officer for the Fortress Study Group.

Dale E Floyd is in the US Army Corps of Engineers and a historian in the office of the Chief of Engineers. He is currently compiling a general bibliography on fortifications and has written widely on American coast defence and Martello towers.

Joan Counihan became interested in Mrs Armitage and *castellogie* about twenty years ago as a mature student studying 'The Norman Conquest' (special subject History BA) under Professor Allen Brown. She has written the entry for Mrs Armitage for the *Dictionary of National Biography.*

Volker Schmidtchen is Professor of Technical and Military History in the University of Witten/Herdeck. President of the Deutsche Gesellshaft für Festungsforsschung in 1981 he is now secretary of the society. Among his many publications on early artillery and fortifications is *Bombarden, Befestigungen, Buchsenmeister* (1977)

Sandy Gerrard. Previously director of excavations at Carew Castle for the Pembrokeshire National Park, Dr Gerrard now works for the Royal Commission on Historical Monuments of England at Southampton.

Correspondence

In response to Paul Huey's letter in *Fortress* 4, David Burridge of Worthing, Sussex writes:

> I read with interest Paul Huey's letter in No 4, since I have often briefly wondered about the same thing. The 'unwritten rule' to which Mr Huey refers appears to have been relaxed somewhat by the time of the 1860 Royal Commission Report. The Report's map of Portsmouth shows 'Elson Fort' and 'Gomer-Fort' but 'Fort Brockhurst', 'Fort Rowner', and 'Fort Grange' (although Dover followed the rule with 'Castle Hill Fort', later renamed 'Fort Burgoyne'). The *History of the Corps of Royal Engineers,* Part III refers to 'Forts Purbrook, Widley, Southwick, Grange, Rowner and Brockhurst' but 'Horse Sand, No Man's Land and Spit Bank Forts', all on the same page. Odd!

Publisher's Note

A small number of issue 5 were returned by the Post Office because the address labels had peeled off. The date and cost of the franking gives us some idea of the intended recipients, but we cannot identify individual subscribers. If any reader did not receive No 5, please contact the publisher.

Back Issues

To enable new subscribers to complete their collection of FORTRESS, the first year's issues are still available. The main features of each are listed below:

FORTRESS 1
Hadrian's Wall/Crusader castles/Bermuda forts/timber castles

FORTRESS 2
Reconstruction drawings of castles/Fortifications of Edessa/Defences of Hull/Defending the sea route to India

FORTRESS 3
Neolithic hillforts/Garrison life at Malta/Channel Island defences/20th century fortifications in East Anglia

FORTRESS 4
Colonial forts around the Indian Ocean/The modern history of Carlisle castle/Arming the Dover Turret/A Czech gun for the Atlantic Wall

FORTRESS 5
Amasra Byzantine Fortress/Transylvanian Fortified Churches/Castellology in Bavaria/Bastle Houses/Crown Point Fort, New York

(£4.50 UK; £5 or $9.50 overseas, per copy)